Prayer

by

James H. McConkey

www.solidchristianbooks.com

2015

Contents

I. THE CALL TO PRAYER.

"Pray ye." – Matt. 9: 38.

The Word of the Father is a call to Prayer.

Everywhere in His Word God calls His children to the prayer life. "Ask, and ye shall receive." "And He spake a parable unto them that men ought always to pray and not to faint." "Pray, that ye enter not into temptation." "Enter into thy closet, shut the door and pray to thy Father." "After this manner therefore pray ye." "Pray ye the Lord of the Harvest." "Pray without ceasing." "Brethren, pray for us." "I will therefore that men pray." "Is any afflicted, let him pray."

The example of the Son is a Call to Prayer.

Christ's earthly life was one of unceasing prayer. He prayed at His baptism. He prayed before sending out His disciples. He prayed at the grave of Lazarus. He prayed for Peter that his faith might not fail He prayed on the Mount of Transfiguration. He prayed when they would have made Him King. He prayed at the last supper. He prayed in Gethsemane. He prayed on the cross for His enemies.

If Christ, the only sinless man who ever walked the earth, lived a life of constant communion with the Father through prayer, how much must we weak, fleshly, earth-bound mortals need it. And not only was

His life here on earth one of unceasing prayer, but that now when He has ascended into the glory we are told "He ever liveth to make intercession." Though we may slumber, and forget, and grow careless in intercession, never in the almost two thousand years that have passed since He went up into the heavenlies, has He for one moment ceased to make intercession for His people and His Kingdom. If Jesus the Son of God is living in the glory in ceaseless intercession, surely we poor earthlings dare not belittle nor disobey His call to us to live with Him the life of prayer.

* * * *

The Drawing of the Spirit is *a Call to Prayer.*

A godly railroad engineer was starting out with his train for the nightly run. The road on which he was running was single track, and at a point about mid-way of his trip he was to meet and pass another train. As his engine plunged forward into the inky darkness he began to think of the oncoming train. Straightway he found himself under a great burden of prayer for the safety of his crew and himself. Try as he would he could not shake off the impression of danger nor the burden of prayer for deliverance from it. "Lord, care for us. Deliver us from any peril that may be threatening us, though unseen," was his petition. All the way from his starting point to the first station, earnestly and trustfully he kept crying to God. Then the burden of supplication changed to one of joy and assurance and he found himself singing as his train swept on. By and by he drew near to the point at which he was to pass the other train. To his surprise the signal for him to stop was not displayed, but instead the white light of safety shone upon the track. Speeding on past the passing station a half hour's run brought him face to face with a glaring danger signal. Entering the telegraph office he found the operator white with fear, and was greeted with the question, "Why did you not stop at A?" naming the station at which he was to have met the other train. "Because there was no signal for me to do so," was his reply." "Well, H-," said the operator, "You have had a desperately narrow escape from death sure." And then the grateful engineer learned that the operator at the station where he was to have met the other train had fallen asleep, and failed to signal his train to stop; that for a half hour the engineer had been running over a piece of track on which the other train was long over-due; but that by a remark able providence this latter train was delayed in starting long enough to prevent the deadly collision which would otherwise have taken place. The same Spirit of God who foresaw the danger had laid upon the heart of His child the burden of prayer concerning it, and then in response to that petition had delivered him from it.

Never disobey this drawing of the Spirit to prayer. It is a special call of God to the individual who is conscious of it. God sees some peril, or great need, in the life or service of one of His own. He chooses some other child to cry to Him concerning it. Tremendous issues may hang upon obedience to that call to prayer. Sad as any neglect of the call to prayer is, the failure to obey this one seems an especial abuse of the grace of God who has honored us by choosing us as His intercessors in such a crisis. Wherefore when you find in your heart this subtle drawing of the Spirit to prayer, steal away and pray it out with God. Some day, even if not in this life, you will see what it meant to God's Kingdom, to some dear friend in need, and to your own spiritual life.

* * * *

Every Need *is a Call to Prayer.*

"For He shall deliver THE NEEDY." – Ps. 72:12.

"It is the needy whom God hears in Prayer. To approach the throne of an eastern king with a petition, one must needs bear costly gifts to win his favor. But ours is a God of grace. "Like as a father pitieth his children, so the Lord pitieth them that fear Him." He asks no gift of gold or gems, But pending down to us in infinite love He says: "My child how needy are you? What heavy burden is upon you? What grievous sorrow is darkening your faith? What fear of future ill is shadowing your pathway? What spiritual thirst do you want slaked? What barrenness of soul enriched? How hungry, how helpless, how faint, how hopeless are you? What do you need this hour? For I will deliver the needy." And so the very need that burdens, dispirits and perplexes us is at once the condition and pledge of His blessing. God's clouds pour refreshing showers upon the sun-parched fields because of their need. God's sun quickens the seed, feeds the plant, and paints the flower because of need. "He shall deliver the needy * * and him that hath no helper." Have you reached a crisis in life where the gloom is so dense, the guidance so uncertain, the burden so heavy, that you have come to the end of all your own resources? You have studied and planned, striven and sought, until baffled at every turn you sink in utter defeat and moan, "There is no help for me; I must give up the fight." Then understand that you are just the man God is looking for – just the one who is ripe for deliverance— just the special individual to whom His promise is made. "For He shall deliver the needy * * and him that hath no helper." Do not be too afraid of getting into the spot where you have no helper, for that is the spot where, like Jacob, you will meet a delivering God. Do not be too anxious to be free from needs, unless you want to be free from prayer-power. Accept them just as sends them or permits them. The moment you come to a need, remember also that you have come to a promise. "He shall deliver the needy." To miss a need may be to miss a miracle. As soon as one appears in your life, do not begin to worry because it is there, but praise God because it is to be supplied.

"For He shall deliver the needy when he crieth."

It is not enough for the soul to be in need. The soul must also cry unto God. Need alone is the begetter of despair. But need with crying is the birth-place of prayer. The very distresses the soul is in are the birth-throes of such prayer. "In my distress I cried unto the Lord." As out of our sorrow we weep, and out of joy, smile, so God means that out of our need we should cry to Him. He does not say He will deliver the needy when he frets, and worries, and schemes – there is no promise for that – but when he cries. Are you daily crying to God? Is prayer the instinctive habit of your soul in need? In distress is the first impulse of your soul to brood? or to cry? Yield not to that, but to this. For that is begotten of the flesh; this born of God. The instant your soul begins to feel the stress of a need, fly to prayer as you would to the well in thirst, or the loaf in hunger. The sign at the railroad crossing is "Stop, look and listen!" So God's sign, set up the moment a need crosses your life's pathway is, cry!

When trouble comes, then "Call upon me in the day of trouble" Ps. 1:15. When in distress, then "In my distress I cried unto my God" Ps. 18:6. When conscious of weakness, helplessness and poverty, then "This poor man cried and the Lord heard * * and saved." Ps. 34:6.

* * * *

Every Anxiety is a Call to Prayer.

Why does our Lord admonish us here against anxiety? And why does He set prayer over against it and warn us: – Be anxious in nothing, but in all things – pray?

Because Anxiety hinders our Faith in God.

For faith is simply looking unto Jesus. It is the helpless, needy, tempted soul, conscious of its own weakness and utter inability to cope with the difficulties all about it, and therefore looking away from all these things to God alone as its source of strength and deliverance. Faith thus looks to God. But anxiety looks to things. Anxiety turns the soul's gaze away from God to the circumstances about us. It causes us to plan and brood about the multitude of things which seek to harass us. In so doing we get our eyes off of God. And this is to lose the attitude of faith. When we look to God, we trust. When we look to things, and circumstances, and surroundings, we grow anxious. "The beginning of

8

anxiety is the end of faith," says Andrew Murray. When we begin to grow anxious faith languishes. "My eyes are ever unto the Lord, and He will pluck my feet out of the net," says the wise Psalmist

So long as he keeps looking unto God, God will take care of the nets and pitfalls which are spread in his pathway. This is the walk of faith. But when he himself begins to try to manage the nets and pitfalls, and look away from God he begins to be filled with anxious care, and this is ruinous to faith.

Anxiety hinders the Power of God.

For faith is the channel through which God's power is poured out upon His children, and in taking us out of the attitude of faith anxiety clogs the downflow of God's power and blessing into our lives. Witness the hindering of Christ's power at Nazareth. We are told that "He could there do no mighty works." And in the literal rendering of this sentence the truth is still more I striking:—"He was there not able to do any mighty work." What was it that the Son of God could not do, and why could He not do it? Why was it that He was hindered and baffled in His desire to do the mighty deeds, as was His wont, here at His own Home? The answer of the Word reveals the secret—"Because of their unbelief" There was something in them that hindered Him. For there is a condition upon our side to Christ's doing mighty deeds for us, and that is that we be in the attitude of faith. Anything which hinders that faith hinders Christ's work. If we are not looking to Him and trusting in Him, the channel through which His power flows to us is closed and He is not able to help us, even though He longs so to do. We wonder sometimes why God does not succor us in our straits. We fear He has left us to ourselves. We are grieved by the seeming hiding of His face. But we do not see that in allowing "The cares of this world" to possess us, we barricade the only pathway over which the power of God travels from heaven to earth to deliver His children. It is not that God is not willing to help us. He is always ready, yea, eager to do that. But He is not able to help us because anxiety had throttled faith, along which alone God is able to act in our behalf.

Anxiety hinders the Peace of God.

In hindering our faith, anxiety not only bars the power of God, but also the peace of God. For peace as well as power comes through faith. "Thou wilt keep him in perfect peace, whose mind is stayed on Thee, because he trusteth in Thee." Peace is here the "because" of trust. And when anxiety attacks trust it banishes peace. Peace is a gentle dove which sits and broods in restful quiet in the heart of the trustful soul. Anxiety is a fierce vulture which tears the heart of its victim with cruel beak and talon until he bleeds away his very life with anxious care. When the vulture of anxiety enters, the dove of peace takes flight. Since the anxiety hinders our faith in God, breaks the power of God and mars our faith in God, is it any wonder that God calls upon us to hasten to prayer as soon as anxiety looms upon our spiritual horizon? Every anxiety becomes a prayer-signal from God. It is like the railroad man's red light. It flashes a warning of danger across our pathway. When anxious care begins to creep into our heart God cries out to us: "Stop! You are going to lose your faith. You are going to shut off my power from your life. You are going to mar my peace in your soul. Beware! There is danger ahead. Fly to prayer. 'Be anxious in nothing, but pray, and my peace shall keep your hearts free from this dread foe of anxious care'"

* * * *

Every Temptation is a call to prayer.

"Watch and pray that ye enter not into temptation." Matt. 26:41. What an awful trio of foes is arrayed against the Christian in temptation. There is the world; the flesh; and the devil. The world – the foe about us: the adversary – the foe beside us: the flesh – the foe within us. All of these combine in fierce assault upon the believer. Take first the World. How many of God's children are swept off their feet by the flood of Worldliness about them. They resist manfully the temptation to the greater sins. They shrink from blasphemy, profanity, or impurity. They would scorn the open allurements of the dram shop, or the house of shame. But myriads of them fall easy and unconscious victims to the ever present worldliness which is the subtlest enemy of the church of Christ to-day. Then think of the power of Satan. How David fell a victim of his wiles. How Peter was charged by out Lord with being an instrument in Satan's hand to try to lure Christ from the path of duty. How fierce was the same adversary's attack upon Job to draw him away from his God. On all sides we see multitudes going down in shameful defeat before the Prince of Evil. No child of God in his own strength is able for one instant to cope with this crafty foe. Only through Christ can he meet him. Dread foes indeed are these two – the world and the prince of this world. But almost more humiliating than either of these is the foe within the fortress, – the Flesh. The outward enemies are bad enough, but when a traitor within betrays us the shame of defeat is but the greater. To feel the scorching breath of the tempter in his fierce onset; to know the swoon of the soul under the awful assault; and then above all to be conscious of that within ourselves which goes out toward sin and reveals to us the hideousness of the Flesh life; all this makes temptation an awful experience for the soul. And in it all there is but one resort. We must fly to our Lord in prayer. None else but Him has ever overcome this trinity of foes embattled against us. Only in His power, through prayer can we prevail. And mark too that the soul needs to fly to Him immediately. Do not first try to meet the enemy in your own strength, and their call on Christ afterwards. Some argue thus: – "God helps those who help themselves. Do the best you can and then call on the Lord when you have failed." A beautiful lesson comes to us from Proverbs 30:26, concerning the danger of such a course. "The conies are a feeble folk, yet they make their houses in the rocks." The cony is a weak, timid little animal like our rabbit or hare. He has no means of defense in himself, so when his foes, the vulture or the eagle, come in sight the cony does not turn at bay and do all he can to defend himself ere he flees. If he did he would be torn to pieces in an instant by his fierce enemies of the air. Nay, the cony has learned a wiser course than this. He knows he is a "feeble folk." So he rushes straight to "The Rocks." He lets the rocks defend him without attempting any defence whatever in his own strength, which is but weakness. Likewise is it with us. We are a feeble folk. We are no match against this triple alliance of the World, the Flesh and the Devil, in temptation. If we would seek to do 'The best we can" in our own strength, we will soon go down in shameful defeat. Our only course is to learn the cony lesson; to fly straight to our Rock, Christ Jesus, in prayer, and trust! the Rock to keep us.

* * * *

Every vision of the world's Unsolvable Problems is a Call to Prayer – Prayer for the coming of our Lord.

"Even so, come, Lord Jesus." Rev. 22:20. Where is the Christian man or woman who has not suffered keenest agony from the vision of the unsolvable problems of this poor suffering World. You go forth to minister among lost men. You do all you can to better their sad estate. You point them to the Christ who taketh away the sin of the world. You show them the pathway of light in which they may walk. You counsel them in their perplexities, comfort them in sorrow, strengthen them in weakness. But when you have done your best, and given yourself, your time, your talent, your all, you are still face to face with problems which are utterly beyond your solution. You stand before them overwhelmed with the consciousness of your own utter helplessness. Your sympathy, your tears, your earnest desire to help, are of no avail. The keenest suffering of the servant of God comes from this vision, of the ills which he himself cannot in any way touch or lighten, much less banish from this poor world. There is Death. It enters the home and takes away the dearest object of our heart's affection. It fills the world with woe unspeakable. It breaks the tenderest ties that link human hearts in one. It spares not our closest flesh and blood. It is the last great enemy yet to be overcome. Before it the bodies of God's most devoted and faithful children, however busy and successful in His service, must go down into the darkness and corruption of the grave. Even the holiest yield this last tribute to its ravages. Then there is sin. What an awful enemy is here. Think of the broken hearts; the wrecked lives; the fathers and mothers who mourn over wayward sons and daughers; the bleeding wounds that all time cannot heal; the burden of care and grief and shame, which has been piling up since the first day when man broke the law of God and the sentence of death fell upon him for sin. Then we can point men to the blood which takes away the guilt of Sin. But what can we do with the problem of Sin in itself, and its existence here?

Again there is Satan. What a subtle and dreadful foe is he. He goeth about like a roaring lion, tempting, deceiving, devouring. How fierce are his onsets; how terrible his power; how cruel and relentless his pursuit of the objects of his wrath and hatred. And then who shall banish cruel oppression? Who shall drive savage War, with all its horrors, from the face of the earth? Who shall stay the ravages of famine, pestilence, and disease? Who shall free this sad world from murder, suicide, hatred, crime? We might almost picture the aged John, in the lonely island of his exile, looking up toward his departed Lord and crying out in his sorrow: "Lord, I can endure thine own absence in the flesh, for

I shall soon see Thee face to face. I can bear the separation from all I loved, for soon I shall be with them. I can endure the loneliness, the suffering, the sadness of it all, for soon my pilgrimage shall end and I shall pass into the glory. I can bear the scorn and contumely of men for these are but part of the tribulation Thou hast promised as my lot here upon earth. But alas for the moan of the world's agony which comes to me as the surge of the sea which breaks upon this lonely shore. Alas, O Lord, for the sorrow, and sin and suffering which all our efforts cannot undo, all our sympathy cannot banish. What canst Thou do for these in our helplessness, O Lord?" And can we not hear our Lord's whisper from the skies above, to His beloved disciple: – "I am coming, John, and when I come all these mysteries shall be solved. When I, the Prince of Peace, shall come, wars shall cease. When I, to whom the Kingdom belongs, shall come, oppression shall end, for the Government shall be upon my shoulders and of the increase of righteousness and peace there shall be no end. When I come the power of Sin shall be broken. When I come the last enemy, Death, shall be put under my feet. When I come Satan shall be bound in darkest dungeon. When I come the darkness shall flee away; the sorrowing shall be comforted; the meek exalted to reign; the broken-hearted healed; the glory of God fill the earth as the waters cover the sea." And with the vision of the glorious triumph of His coming Lord over the evil, and sin, and gloom, and pain, and of His triumphant solution of all those awful problems which well nigh break the heart of His children who serve Him here, is there any wonder that, in an ecstasy of joy at the blessed promise "Lo I come quickly," John should breathe the last great prayer of the Word of God: –

"EVEN SO, COME, LORD JESUS."

II. THE CERTAINTY OF PRAYER.

"Every one * * receiveth." – Matt 7:7, 8, 11; Matt 6:8.

* * * *

As we hear the call of God and enter into the closet of prayer, the first great truth with which He confronts us is that of the Certainty of Prayer as set forth in the words: –

"EVERY ONE THAT ASKETH RECEIVETH."

Notice at the very outset that Christ does not say everyone that asketh receiveth the very thing he asks for. We read this into it, but Christ does not say it. For it is not true.

It is not true in our experience. Many a time we have asked for things which we have not received. And often have we been sorely puzzled and made to stumble by the seeming clash between this verse and our own failure to get everything for which we asked. Neither is it true in the Word of God. Notice how guarded our Lord is against saying, in this passage, that everyone who asks receives the very thing he asks for. He does say, "Everyone that asks receives" – but there He stops. And "He that seeketh findeth" – but again He pauses. And why does He, in His wisdom, stop short of saying that the asker receives the thing he asks for, and the seeker the very thing for which he seeks? bet us note in answering, that our Lord is here instructing beginners in the prayer life. He is teaching the A B C of prayer. He is giving His first great lesson to those who sit upon the primary benches in this great school of prayer. And the worst thing which could happen to a beginner in the prayer life would be to teach him that he would receive everything he asked for.

How clear this is with the earthly child. Here comes the little one and asks papa for the knife, or the razor. He knows what he wants, but he does not know what is best; he does not know that these would mean mutilation and suffering for him. He asks all amiss when he asks for them, and his father, knowing this, does not give them. To give a boy all the money he wants, just the companions he wants, and as little education as he wants, would be the surest way possible to wreck his life. The most ruinous thing in the world is for a parent to give a son everything he desires. Some call that parental love, whereas it is only parental weakness mistaking indulgence for love. Real love, such as God's, gives not always what is wanted, but what is best. We ought to be just as grateful to the God who does not give us everything according to our will as we are to the God who does give us everything according to His will. Is not that true in the life of your child at the beginning? Is it not true in our life? What we want to have and what God wants to give meet in beautiful harmony when we come to live our lives in the will of God. For then we desire only what God wills, and then God can and does give gladly to us "all things whatsoever we desire." But at the beginning of our Christian life we are not thus wholly in the will of God. There is much of self-will and selfish desire in us, and it would be ruinous for God to give us everything we asked while our life was under the mastership of self. Thus it is that our Lord in His first great teaching of the truth of the prayer-life, while He does say that "Everyone that asks receives," carefully guards Himself against saying that he always receives the thing he asks for.

Observe also that Christ does not say anything about asking according to the will of God. He does not mention the great promise of John's Gospel, that if we ask anything according to God's will we will get that very thing. Or that if we abide in Him, and He in us, we shall ask whatsoever we will and it shall be given. All this is true. But it is not what Christ is teaching here. It is not the truth for beginners in the life of supplication. And why? Because a child whose receiving was conditioned upon always asking according to the will of his father or mother, would soon become discouraged thereat. He might well say, "If I can only receive from God when I know His will, then I cannot enter into the prayer-life. For often God's will is a mystery, and often I come to God not knowing that will. And therefore if prayer has blessing for me only when I am praying according to God's will, I am afraid it is not until I get to be a far more mature Christian that I can begin to pray." What then is our Lord here teaching? Simply this, that

Every one that asks receives – something.

He is teaching the certainty of all prayer. He is teaching that not only the man who is asking according to the will of God receives the thing he asks for, but that every child of God who prays receives something in the place of prayer. He is teaching that all prayer brings blessing.

In the profoundest sense there is no unanswered prayer. The closet of prayer is God's distributing station. He turns no one away empty-handed. Entirely apart from the question of receiving the thing we ask for, there are general blessings in prayer which God gives to everyone who comes into the place of prayer.

It is as though a little lad came to mamma and said, "Mamma, whenever I come to papa he does not always give me the thing I ask for, but he always gives me something. And he tells me to always come to him in my troubles and that he will always help." Now is not this just the lesson the beginner in the prayer-life needs? Our Father is saying: "Come, my child, into the closet of prayer. For everyone who comes there shall receive. Though you may not yet knew how to ask according to My will, yet you shall receive. Though you may not yet have learned how to abide in Me, yet you shall receive. Though you may not yet knew how to pray as you ought, you shall receive – something. Every time you come I am here to give." What an encouragement this promise is to the child of God who, as a beginner in prayer, is weak, or timid, or ignorant. It is the very promise above all others that would encourage him to enter into the blessed school of prayer to which a loving Father is inviting him.

* * * *

Everyone that asks receives – good things.

"How much more shall your Father which is in heaven give good things to them that ask Him?" (Matt. 7:11.) That is, apart from the particular petition we may put up in prayer, God has a store of general blessings and gifts, of "good things" which He gives to all who pray, even where they may not get the special thing for which they ask. It is as though we come to a store and ask the merchant for something. He refuses, saying he does not have it for us. But then and there he loads us up with the choicest silks and satins, gold and silver and jewels and precious stones, and sends us away with our hands full of richest gifts. Have we not received from him? Although he may not have given us the thing we asked for, he has given us good things, worth, perhaps, a great deal more than that for which we asked. So whether we get the thing we asked for or not – which we will do when we come to abide in Him – God always gives "good things." So used have we been to thinking that the only answer in prayer is to get the exact thing we ask, that we have overlooked the preciousness of these general blessings of all prayer. Let us now note some of these "good things... In the first place in prayer, God gives:

Light.

"Call unto Me * * and I will show thee" (Jer. 33:3). The closet of prayer is a chamber of revelation. Nowhere else do we receive light from God as there. For there we hear voices heard not elsewhere. Here are outflashings of truth as nowhere else. Here the Spirit illumines some passages of Scripture for our guidance as in no other place. It is like going into an unlighted room where every object is veiled in darkness. You know not where or how to walk. But presently you touch a little button, and straightway from every nook and corner in the room shines forth the light of the incandescent lamps hidden

21

therein. So when in darkness and perplexity you are seeking guidance, it is as you pray that the light flashes upon you and the way is made clear.

How dark was the way to Peter, with his mind dominated by Jewish prejudices, and not knowing that God wanted the Gospel given to the Gentiles. It was as he was praying on the housetop that God opened the heavens and gave him the light of that great vision. It was as Paul was praying that God said, "Arise, go into the city, and it shall be shown thee... It was as he was praying again that Ananias came to him and touched his eyes, and he received his sight. It was as Cornelius prayed that God gave him the guidance that finally brought him into the light of the gospel of God in the face of Jesus Christ. When Christian and Hopeful fell into Doubting Castle, they lay there for four days in darkness and despair. Then it suddenly came to Christian, "Let us go to prayer." And the narrative tells us that as they prayed on until near the morning, it flashed upon Christian, "Why, I have a key that will let us out," and, taking it from his bosom, in a few minutes they were in the place of deliverance. It was when they prayed that light came, and not before.

Again in prayer (2 Cor. 12:8, 9) God gives

Submission.

Sometimes we ask for something which is not according to God's will. Then as we pray, it is in the midst of our prayer that we are led to give up our own will, and come into humble submission to God's better will. That was so with Paul. He prayed three times and God did not give the thing he asked for, but God gave submission to His will and abounding grace for the weakness which remained. We do not understand the mystery of Gethsemane, and dare hardly comment on it. But we do see this, that at the beginning there was a "Thy will" and "My will," for He said, "Not My will but Thine" At the end there was only "Thy will be done." What is the mystery of our Lord's struggle there? We do not know, but where its beginning was petition, its end was submission. You and I have gone into the place of prayer with the life of some loved one trembling in the balance. How hard it was for us to ask anything else than that I God might spare that loved one. We prayed on and on, and as we prayed we saw that this might not be His will. But as we saw that, instead of rebellion, we found God pouring out upon us a conscious spirit of submission. Then and there we said, "Thy will be done." If we had no other blessing in prayer, this alone would be enough. For there is no more precious blessing in all life than that of a will wholly yielded to God. And this comes in prayer, whether we receive the specific thing we are asking for or not.

Another one of the "good things" God gives in prayer is:

Peace.

Recall here the familiar passage of Philippians 4:6, 7, "In nothing be anxious; but in everything by prayer and supplication with thanksgiving, let your requests be made known unto God. And the peace of God * * * shall guard your hearts." God does not say, "Be anxious for nothing, but bring all things to Me with prayer and supplication, and I will give you just what you ask." But what does He say? "The peace of God shall guard your hearts and your thoughts in Christ Jesus."

What is the Lord teaching us here? Simply this. Our anxious care about burdens is due to our bearing them ourselves. But if we take these burdens to God in prayer and lay them upon Him, He will give us peace. This then is one of the great general blessings, one of the "good things" of prayer—that it brings us peace in our very habit of bringing to, and laying upon another, even God, the burdens and anxieties which have been robbing us of peace because we were carrying the load ourselves. The chamber of prayer is the birthplace of Peace.

Too often we think the peace of God some ecstatic blessing which falls out of heaven without any fulfilled condition on our part. And we wonder why it does not come to fill us all the time. But there is a human side to this, and it is that we are to take all things to God in prayer. As the little child's habit of running to mamma with every anxiety however trifling is what gives it peace, so the child of God finds the peace of God through coming to Him in the same way. If we are to have the peace of God at all times we must come to Him in prayer with all things. And what then is the promise? The peace of God shall "garrison"—that is the word in the Greek – our hearts. How beautiful! The army in the field camps, one night here, and is gone the next day miles away. It camps again and the next day flits to another spot, moving hither and thither. But a garrison settles down in a fort and stays there all the time. Now if we will bring to God everything in prayer the peace of God will garrison our hearts; it will stay, it will abide there. The habit of prayer will bring abidingness of Peace.

Then again, and lastly, in prayer God gives:

The Holy Spirit.

"If ye then, being evil, know how to give good gifts unto your children, how much more shall your Heavenly Father give the Holy Spirit to them that ask Him" (Lu. 11:13). Not that God's children have not received the Holy Spirit at regeneration. They surely have, for "if any man have not the Spirit of Christ he is none of His." But it is not enough for a child to receive life at birth. There must also be daily food for the sustaining of that life. And so the fact that God here says "children" proves that He is talking of those who have already received His gift of life in the Spirit. And the words "fish," "bread" and "egg," food for the daily supply of needs, seem to plainly show that He is speaking of that daily refreshing and anointing by His Spirit which every child of His needs, as much as he needs the daily food to sustain his physical life. "One baptism; many anointings," is the dual truth here. It is one thing to have the Spirit in us. It is another thing for us to be daily and hourly "in the Spirit." And this is just what prayer does for us. It brings the anointing, the unction, the daily touch of the Spirit of God upon our lives. If there is one thing we are conscious of when we rise from our knees at prayer it is that the Spirit of God has touched us. Prayer puts us "in the Spirit" as nothing else does. And what greater blessing could it bring than that? For when we are in the Spirit we will not speak harsh or caustic words: in the Spirit we will not rebuke people except in love: in the Spirit we will not walk in the lusts of the flesh: in the Spirit we will do the works of the Spirit; will bear the brand of the Spirit; will be filled with the love, joy and peace of the Spirit; will be led and guided and comforted by the Spirit. There is no greater blessing that prayer could bring to us than to put us in the Spirit, and when Christ gives us this passage, "How much more shall your Heavenly Father give the Holy Spirit to them that ask Him," He utters it as though that were the gift in prayer that took in all else, the supreme equivalent of all the other "good things" which everyone that asks receives.

Everyone that asks receives – the very Thing HE NEEDS.

"For your Father knoweth what things ye have need of before ye ask Him" (Matt. 6:8). Not only as we ask does God give us something, not only does he give us "good things," but He gives us the very thing we need. "Your Heavenly Father knoweth what things ye have need of before ye ask Him." "My God shall supply all your need." God always gives us the very thing that we need in prayer, whether we get the thing we ask for or not. What more could we want than this? Prayer is the soul's cry to God to meet some great need. The particular petition put up is only the soul's interpretation of that need. But the soul may be mistaken in this interpretation, for it is often conscious of need, but fails in coming to God in prayer to rightly translate that need into petition. So God looks deeper than the words upon the lips and meets the secret need of the life, which is the real, even though unconscious, cry of the heart. That cry of the heart is real prayer. The word of the lip is often only our mistranslation of it. We know not how to pray as we ought. Thus there may be unanswered petition, but in the profoundest sense there is never any unanswered prayer.

We close with an illustration: Several summers ago, with body broken in health, we were spending the vacation time on the shores of the great lakes. On account of physical weakness sailing was the only recreation possible. Day after day we sailed the beautiful bay and under the blessing of God were slowly regaining the lost strength. One day when sailing in the midst of the bay the wind suddenly died out. Our boat was utterly becalmed, with not a breath of air astir. The surface of the bay was like a mirror, so still and motionless. The hot rays of the August sun beat down upon the weak body, and we knew that unless help soon came we would be in desperate straits indeed. We had come out with a stiff, fresh breeze, and naturally we began to pray for a breeze to take us back. We prayed and prayed for an hour for a breeze, but none came. The bay still lay like a mirror, motionless, the water not roughened by a single ripple. But by and by over toward the shore we espied a black speck creeping around the point that projected out into the channel from the village whence we had started. It came nearer and nearer and soon disclosed the bent form and the whitened head of the old fisherman host with whom we were staying. As he drew near we greeted him with, "Well, Grandfather, I am glad to see you. What brought you here anyhow?" "Well," he said, "I knew you were not strong and could never row that great boat in to shore, so I felt as though I ought to come out and search for you, and here I am." He got into the boat, and bending his sturdy form to the ash oars, in twenty minutes we were safe in the quiet of our own room. Then and there the Lord taught us a lesson. We had prayed for a breeze. God had denied the words of our petition, but the real prayer of our heart was for Deliverance, and that God had heard and signally answered. Let us be thankful for the God who always gives when it is best. Let us be grateful also for the God who refuses when it is not best. We would not have any other kind of a God if we could. We could not trust any other kind of a God if we would. Thank God that though we may make mistakes in asking, God never makes any mistakes in giving. He may fail to give us the thing we ask, but He never fails to give us something. And if that something is better than we ask, and always the very thing we most need, what more could we desire? Would we have it otherwise? Behold, even for the veriest beginner, the certainty of all prayer in these great promises of God.

"Everyone that asketh receiveth" – *something.*

Everyone that asketh receiveth – good things.

Everyone that asketh receiveth – the very thing he needs.

Everyone that asketh according to God's will – receiveth the very thing he asks for.

III. THE GREAT PROMISE.

If ye shall ask anything in my name I will do it (John 14:14.)

* * * *

How often a verse of Scripture seems to be a sealed treasure. You read it again and again but it is padlocked against you. No light breaks from its recesses as you search. But some day, all unexpectedly to yourself, it suddenly opens and discloses its beauties, even as a jewel casket might unclose under the touch of a secret spring and lay bare in an instant all the radiance and loveliness of the priceless gem that lies within. Just so as you let the Spirit of truth lift out from the heart of this passage the condition "In my name" note the precious jewel of truth which is laid bare thereby. Not that this condition is not needful. It is always and absolutely so. For no suppliant can come to God and be heard in prayer save as he comes in the name of our Lord. But assuming now that this condition is fulfilled in our petition and that we are asking in His name and for that which is according to His will. Then there stands forth from the heart of this verse these wondrous words

"IF YE ASK... I WILL, DO."

Consider the wondereulness of this *Promise*

Many and precious are the other promises which God gives to His praying children. He tells us that as we pray and receive our joy shall be full, (Jno. 16:24); that if we bring all things to Him in prayer His own unspeakable peace shall possess and keep our hearts in Christ Jesus, (Phil. 4:7); that of all who ask from Him not one shall be turned away; that to any who knock at His door it shall without fail be opened, (Matt. 7:7, 8). Familiar enough and gracious too is His truth that as we ask He gives. So says His Word again and again: "Ask and it shall be given you;" "Every one that asketh receiveth, "How much more will your Heavenly Father give good things to them that ask Him". But here in the heart of this great chapter, we come upon the greatest promise God has ever given to His praying children. Presuming that the child of God is asking in His name, or according; to His will, the wondrous statement is here made that not only as we pray does God give, but that

AS WE PRAY GOD WORKS.

God, the eternal God of the universe stands, as it were, like an almighty servant and says: "If you, my child, will only pray I will *work;* if you will only be busy with asking I will see to the doing". Not only does He bestow at our cry, but He acts. Not only does our prayer evoke His bounty, it sets in motion His omnipotence. Wherefore, as we enter into the secret chamber of prayer, nothing will so stir us to mighty intercession, nothing will so soon make us master-pleaders with God for a lost world, as to whisper to our own soul, again and again, this wonderful truth, *"While I am praying God is really doing that which I am asking!"*

Thus to a child of God bowed in prayer that the gospel may be sent to the dark lands, though he may not see it, yet as he prays God baffles the powers of darkness; as he prays God moves the hearts of kings; as he prays God breaks down the barriers to evangelization; as he prays God loosens the bands of superstition; as he prays God opens up the pathways to forbidden lands; as he prays God unclasps the purses of His children; as he prays God raises up and thrusts forth the gospel messengers to the whitened harvests. As he is praying God is doing. This is explicitly asserted. "Search my word," says our Lord. Find out clearly in it what my will is concerning the world. Pray according to that will. Then as you pray "Lord thrust forth laborers into the harvest," I thrust them forth! As you pray "Lord break down the obstacles," I break them down! As you pray "Lord stir men's hearts to give," I stir them! Whatsoever ye ask in my name, I do." Beloved, what a tremendous responsibility is ours! What a unique privilege! That all the power of an omnipotent God is ready and waiting to be put into triumphant, irresistible action at the prayer of one of His children! That the very hosts of heaven are marshalled against the powers of darkness at that importunate call of yours which is according to the will of God! He declares that all power in heaven and earth is His, and then, as it were, places Himself at our disposal and says, "Now my child you pray and I will work; you ask and I will do." As an engineer might suffer a child, powerless in itself, to call forth mighty power, not its own, by opening the throttle of his great machine, so God says to us weaklings, "All power is mine, but unto you it is given to call it forth by prayer," If it be true, then, that God's omnipotence is placed at our disposal, we are as responsible for its exercise through prayer as though we possessed it ourselves.

31

Behold here the shame of an unevangelized world, of two thousand years delay, of our cowardice and faltering in the presence of difficulties. For though we have had no power to do, yet the mighty God, linking Himself with us as a real yoke-fellow and coworker, has said

"IF YE ASK I WILL DO."

* * * *

Consider the need of this Promise.

Notice the working of God in human hearts, in answer to prayer, as the great secret of power in the apostolic church. It was God who poured out the Holy Spirit upon the waiting multitude; it was God who wrought conviction in the three thousand which made them cry out in agony of heart "Men and brethren, what shall we do?" It was the Lord which added to the church daily such as were being saved; it was the Lord who healed the lame man through the word of Peter: "In the name of Jesus Christ of Nazareth rise up and walk" were the words with which Peter greeted him. It was the Lord who stretched forth His hand to heal and to do signs and wonders in the name of His holy child Jesus"; it was the Lord to whom Ananias and his wife are said to have lied and not to men; it was the angel of the Lord who opened the prison and brought forth the disciples; it was the Lord who sent Philip down into the desert; it was the Lord who said, "Go near and join thyself to the chariot;" it was the Lord who met Saul in the road, and his word was, "Lord, what wilt thou have me to do?" And again, when Ananias came to him he said, "Brother Saul, the

Lord hath sent me." Notice the Lord working with Peter and Cornelius. He fairly manipulates them as one might manipulate figures upon a stage. It was the Lord who drew Peter aside to prayer; it was the Lord who let down the sheet from heaven and spoke to him; it was the Lord who said, "Go with the men fearing nothing," and it was the Lord who fell upon the waiting multitude at the house of Cornelius as they listened to Peter's message. So also in our own day. Charles Finney so realized the need of God's working in all his service that he was wont to send the godly Father Nash on in advance to pray down the power of God into the meetings which he was about to hold David Brainerd prayed eight days in the wilderness for the working of God's Spirit among the Indians, and hundreds were brought to Christ in answer to his asking. In the great Irish revival of a half century ago, the most striking feature was the working of God's Spirit in the hearts of men. Conviction fell upon men in street, field, and forest, and the church stood in awe at the wonderful work of God in the hearts of lost men. And all this in answer to the prayers of His children.

How we need this same mighty doing of God in our own midst to-day. We need it in the pulpit; we need it in the mission field; we need it in the hearts of the unsaved; we need it in our own lives as God's servants. We need it in the church of Jesus Christ as much as of old. Revivals are sadly infrequent. Strong conviction in the hearts of men bowing them down with deep contrition of soul is almost a thing of the past. The form of godliness without the power thereof is more and more prevalent. The clang of machinery is heard everywhere in the church's work, but not the sound of the rushing mighty wind. There are many tongues of utterance but the tongue of fire is rare. The church is the most highly organized machine in existence. But "a machine is an instrument for the transmission of power." If there is no power, of what avail is the machine? "Power belongeth unto God." It flows down from God to us through prayer. Therefore prayerlessness is powerlessness.

"We may appoint the evangelistic meeting, call the evangelist; train the great choir of voices; organize and equip the meeting in every detail; advertise the service; crowd the auditorium with listeners to the preached Word—but, if the power of God does not fall upon preacher and people, if the Spirit of God does not work in the hearts of the lost; if the presence of God is not seen and felt in the assembled multitude our efforts are in vain. God's power alone is equal to the crisis which every lost soul confronts in the time of decision which follows the preaching of His Word. "Why could not we cast him out?" said the diciples to our Lord concerning the demon who possessed the suffering child. And so we find ourselves saying: Why cannot we cast out the demons of drink and impurity from men? Why cannot we accomplish mighty results in the sphere in which God has placed us? The answer is found in the very terms of the question – because "we" are trying to do it in our own power. We think it is our energy; our plans and efforts; our wisdom; our power that is to bring things to pass. And some day we waken up to find the power gone and the fruitfulness missing and the blessing lost from our lives, and we say as the apostle said, Why cannot we do these things? And back to us comes the same answer our Lord gave to the failure of His disciples, "Have faith in GOD." As though He said: "YOU cannot cast out devils, nor do anything else, in your own strength. It is GOD alone who can do these things. But if you will learn the secret of the prayer life and come to Him, then, though yon yourselves cannot do and are never, in your own strength, meant to do, He fulfils His great promise:

"If – ye – ask – I – will – do."

* * * *

Consider the privilege: of this *Promise.*

If you were weary and despondent and wished to be soothed and cheered by the sweet influence of music, what a privilege you would consider it to have a Mozart, a Beethoven, or a Liszt soothe your tired nerves with ravishing melodies simply because you had asked them. If you had some dear friend, the memory of whose face you wished to treasure upon canvass, what a privilege you would reckon it, at your merest request, to have a Raphael, or a Reynolds, or a Van Dyke paint that face with masterful skill. To have such masters come and do for you because you had asked would indeed be accounted a rare and gracious privilege.

But who is it here who offers to do for us, if we will only ask? It is no untried apprentice, no bungling worker accustomed to failure. It is God Himself. It is the mightiest doer in the universe who says "I will do, if you ask." Unrivalled wisdom, boundless skill, limitless power, infinite resources are His. Think a moment who

35

it is that promises. He who shrouded the land of Egypt in awful darkness; He who turned her streams of water to streams of blood; He who laid His hand upon her first-born and filled her borders with mourning; He who broke the stubborn will of her impious king; He who led forth His people Israel, with mighty arm and outstretched hand; He who parted the great sea, and made the glassy walls of water to be bulwarks of safety to them, and swift avalanches of death to their pursuing foes; He who, when His children cried for water, sweetened the bitter wells to quench their thirst; He who, when they hungered sent them bread from heaven; He who, when they marched about Jericho in utter selfhelplessness, leveled its towering walls by the word of His power; He who walked with His three children in the fierce, fiery furnace, yet kept them even from the smell of scorching garments; He who stilled the tempest, walked on the seas, cast out devils, healed the living and raised the dead – it is this same mighty doer who says He will do for me, if I ask! This omnipotence is the very same omnipotence whose doing is awaiting my praying!

Yea the God who holds the sea in the hollow of His hand; the God who swings this ponderous globe of earth in its orbit more easily than you could swing a child's toy rubber ball; the God who marshals the stars and guides the planets in their blazing paths with undeviating accuracy; the God of Sinai, and of Horeb; the heaven-creating, devil-conquering, dead-raising God, – it is this very God who says to you and to me:

Consider the sureness of the *Promise*.

God does not say "If ye ask perchance I shall do"; or, "If ye ask I may do"; but "If ye ask. Will, do." It is Satan alone who tempts us to question this "I will" of God's prayer promise: to doubt whether God will really hear and answer us as He has answered others in times past. Just so did he tempt Adam and Eve to doubt God's word: "In the day thou eatest thereof thou Shalt surely die." But God's "I will" of promise to us is just as sure as God's "Thou Shalt" of punishment was to them. Over against Satan's subtle lies let us ever place the eternal certainty of these blessed words of promise "I will do." Steadfast and sure is His word of promise. "Though it seems to you difficult, yea impossible, to be done, yet if ye ask I will do. Though for reasons of love and child-training I long delay, yet if ye ask I will do. Though Satan resists with fierce and desperate opposition, yet if ye ask I will do. Though ye are in dire need, I will supply that need if ye but ask. Though ye walk in darkness and know not the way before you, yet I will guide you if ye but ask. Though the obstacles are many, and the hearts of my children slow to obey, yet I will thrust forth laborers into the dark lands if we but ask in faith

In all ages God has made this word "If ye ask I will do" to be true to His children. How sure it was with Peter when the young church prayed for his deliverance from the hand of Herod. How they must have feared as they prayed; how they must have thought of the iron-bound gates, the massive walls, the vigilant and ever present guards. Yet God's word was true. When they prayed, God did. When they asked, the gates swung open to an unseen hand, the prison was shaken by an unseen power, and the astonished disciple was led forth by a ministering angel from the God Himself who did as His people asked. Perhaps Elijah trembled at the thought of closing the doors of heaven by his own petitioning. Yet God's word was sure to him too. When he asked, God did for him, and the skies became as brass over the parched and rainless earth. Again he asked and still God did, and the heavens were opened and flooded that same earth with showers of blessing. Daniel asked and God did by showing him the wondrous vision of His people's coming King. Hezekiah asked and God did by driving back the host of the Syrians, smiting thousands of them by the hand of his death angel. The disciples asked for boldness and God did by pouring out the Holy Spirit in abundant power, "And they spake the Word with boldness." Charles Finney asked and God did, by smiting men with heart-searching conviction under the mighty power of His servant's messages. George Muller asked and God did, by building orphanages; supporting thousands of parentless children through faith alone, and sending in all over thirty thousand answers to prayer to this godly servant. Hudson Taylor asked and God did, by founding, sustaining, and marvelously blessing one of the greatest missionary enterprises the world has ever seen, through the power of believing prayer alone. John G. Paton asked and God did in all the record of his deliverances and blessings among the savages of the New Hebrides. Jacob Chamberlain asked in the jungles of India, in deadly peril from rising flood, and God whispered words of guidance to his inmost soul, led him to the banks of the flooded Godavari, loosed a boat from its moorings ten miles above, and gave passage and deliverance to his servants by a veritable miracle in the heart of India. In all ages has our God been true to this blessed prayer promise.

No word of His has ever failed nor ever shall. When Elijah prayed for rain it was just as sure as when the waiting heavens began to pour forth their torrents. When the church prayed for Peter's deliverance it was as sure as when the barred gates clanged open and the angel of deliverance was walking by his side. Let these wondrous words "I will, do" ring in our ears day after day until deep down in our heart of hearts we shall have no shadow of doubt that an omnipotent God stands pledged and ready to work mighty deeds for us if we will but believingly ask that which is according to His divine will.

* * * *

Consider the simplicity of the *Promise.*

God does not say to us: "If ye win my favor by good works I will do"; or, "If ye bring sacrifices or burnt offerings to my altar I will do;" "If ye make me rich gifts of silver and gold I will do." But simply, "If ye ask I will do" The way to get a thing which is sold is to pay for it; the way to get a thing which is earned is to work for it; the way to get a thing which is given is to ask for it. We live in an age of grace. God's method of blessing His children is not to sell but to give. God's plan for them to receive, is not to buy nor to earn, but only to ask. The very simplicity of this causes us to stumble. We are like Naaman the leper. When told to go and wash in Jordan, he was insulted and refused. "Why does not the prophet come forth and do some great thing? Why does he not

39

stretch forth his hand and bid the disease depart? Why does he ask me to do so simple an act as to go wash in the Jordan? Are there not rivers in Damascus far better than this?" And he was about to depart in a rage. Then wise advisers counseled him thus: "If the prophet had bidden thee do some great thing, would'st thou not have done it? Why not go wash then in the Jordan?" And he went, and washed and was made clean. Just so with us. If God's blessings came to us by purchase, we would work day and night for the gold and silver wherewith to buy them. If they came to us through our own deeds of merit we would climb many a St. Peter's staircase, and toil our weary way to many a distant Mecca to win them. But because God's mighty doing for us is conditioned on our simple asking we stumble thereat fail to find the blessing he has in store for those who simply ask.

Dr. Gordon tells of a little child in one of the New England States who fell and broke her arm. Her father was a physician, and after he had set the broken member, the little one said to him "Papa, can you cure it for me?" "No, my child, I cannot do any more for it." "Well, papa, I am going to ask Jesus to cure it," to which the father gave a smiling, but doubtful assent. That night the little one in her evening prayer, put up a simple request to the Lord Jesus to heal the broken arm. The next morning she came in triumph to her astonished and awe-stricken father and showed him her arm made perfectly whole. Would not our Lord have more of such simple faith in us His children? We who know so much that we would not do a thing like this, is not our wisdom that wisdom of men which is foolishness with God? We have grown so wise we have forgotten how to trust. We are so self-dependent that we do not know the power and blessing of utter dependence on God. "Except ye become as little children ye cannot enter into the kingdom of God. Except we live like such we cannot know the secrets of its blessedness. God wants us to go in and out before Him as a little child goes in and out of its father's house, asking for what we need and for what will glorify God in the most artless and childlike faith that God will surely give it. So doing our service for Him may not be so fussy, pretentious and feverish as much of modern religious activity is, but it will have the fragrance, simplicity and divine anointing that can flow only from Him who lives a life of prayer and childlike trust in God his Father, and who trusts implicitly in His great promise:

"If ye ask I will do."

* * * *

Consider the personalness of this *Promise.*

In James 5:17, the Word of God, after telling us of the wonderful prayer-life of Elijah: how he had through prayer shut up the heavens until they were as brass, and then how by the same simple faith in God he had opened them so that they poured forth rain in floods upon the drouth-smitten earth, goes on to use these words: "Elijah was a man of like nature (R. V.) with us" And what is it that is meant here? Simply this, The Holy Ghost who wrote this book, knew that when we read the narrative of the wondrous deeds wrought by Elijah through prayer, we would, in the weakness of our faith, be saying: "Ah, yes; it is all right for a man like Elijah to

41

expect wonderful answers to his prayers; but I am not an Elijah, and I cannot expect God to do great things for me in the prayer life. And so God puts in this narrative those striking words of rebuke to our unfaith. He says in effect: "Elijah was a flesh and blood a man just like you, and if you come to Me with the same simple faith I will do wondrous things for you as well as for him. Not only when Elijah, or Moses, or Paul, asked did I do, but if ye ask I will do for you. There was not anything in the nature of Elijah different from yours. It was not that Elijah himself was a wonderful man. But he trusted in a wonderful God. And if you do the same and ask with the same faith I will do great things for you."

A godly woman, mother of six children, had come into a place of great stress. Her husband, absent in a distant city earning the livelihood, had been unfortunate; the needed remittances had failed to come to the wife and family, and their last loaf of bread had been eaten at the evening meal. The next morning, without a morsel of food in the house, the trustful mother set the table with seven plates, and gathering the children about her, said : "And now children we must ask God to supply our need." As she finished her petition for help one of the little ones cried out, "There is the baker at the door." Immediately his knock was heard, and entering, he said, "I was stalled in the snow this morning and thought I would come in to get warm. By the way do you need any bread this morning?" "Yes," said the mother, "but we have no money to buy any." "What?" said the baker, as he glanced at the empty plates and took in the situation, "do you mean to say you have no bread for these children?" "Not a morsel," said the mother. "Well, you shall soon have some," said the kindhearted man, and going out quickly to his wagon he returned with seven loaves of bread and laid one at each plate. Thereupon, one of the little children, picking up a loaf in his arms, dancing around the room, crying out, "Mamma, I prayed for bread and God heard me, and sent me bread." "And me!" "And me!" chorused the rest of the glad-hearted little folk. Each one of the little ones felt that God heard him personally and sent a loaf to him directly and individually. And was it not true?

Even so does our Father in heaven deal with us His children if we but trust Him. He does not say "It is only the great ones of the kingdom of heaven whom I hear and answer; only the Elijahs and Daniels, the Elishas and Pauls. But in His great promise of prayer to us He puts that little word "YE," and says it to all His children who will believe Him. "YE" pastors whose work must be a failure without the convicting power of God upon your people; who need yourself the anointing of God's Spirit for the mighty preaching of the Word; who are deeply conscious of the need of God's working through prayer if your work is not to be fruitless. "YE" missionaries who are contending against the awful powers of darkness in heathendom; meeting the fierce wrath of the adversary at every turn; conscious of his deadly assaults upon your own inner life; seeing the sin and blackness of the human heart as none of the rest of us do; face to face with problems which only God can solve. "YE" who have loved ones outside of Christ, who are daily resisting His call; who are going down to eternal death unless God works in their hearts through prayer. "YE," who serve the Lord and realize the need of His quickening power in all that you say and do. YE, who are burdened with anxious care; YE, who walk in dark ness and have no light; YE, who are high or low rich or poor, learned or ignorant, it matters not, to all you His children, He says

"If ye ask I will do for you."

IV. THE SWEEP OF PRAYER.

"If ye shall ask ANYTHING in my name I will do it" – Jno. 14:14-

* * * *

If we ask, God will do in our needs.

A striking ilustration of this recently came un-der our notice. Walking one evening in the park of a great health resort we met a Christian woman in great distress of soul, who, opening her heart, poured out this story of her trouble. "I am," said she, "the only daughter of a widowed mother, wholly dependent upon me for support. All these years it has been my privilege and joy to care for her and minister to her modest needs. A few months ago my health failed and I was driven to this sanitorium in the hope of restoration. The little store of money I had with me has melted away, and I do not have enough to pay the bills now due. Moreover, day after to-morrow I must pass through a critical operation which may mean death. I am not concerned about myself, for my peace with God is made. But if I should die under this operation there is not one soul in all this world to care for the mother whom I love more than I love my own life," and then she burst into tears and sobbed out her agony of sorrow and apprehension the dark and uncertain future before her tried to comfort her by God's word of promise that He would hear her prayer and supply her need if she but called upon Him and looked trustfully to Him to answer* quoting to her the promise "My God shall supply all your need." "Ah," she said, "I know nothing about that. I have always been accustomed to earning my own living with my own hands and brain. Now that I have come to the end of my self, such a thing as God answering prayer and supplying my need, direct from His own heart of love for a helpless child of His, is an unknown experience. Why, my dear friend, I have never known what it was to have a direct answer to prayer from God, such as you say He will give if I call upon Him in faith." We earnestly pressed upon her the truth that God was her loving Heavenly Father, and that He would not only supply her needs through the labor of her hands, but was pledged to supply them when she was disabled from using her own efforts if she would only commit her way unto the Lord," and call upon Him in the trust of a little child. At last she yielded to the truth and the drawing of God's Spirit in her own heart. She committed to Him the dark ominous future; the dreaded operation with its possible outcome of death; the beloved mother, her own pressing needs, yea, her very self and all that concerned herin time or eternity. And then we called on concerning her urgent financial needs, pleading. His promise "My God shall supply all your need;" and "If ye ask, I will do;" and parted.

Two days later, on the morning of the operation, we were hastening to our room to fulfil the promise made to hold her up in prayer at the moment of her supreme crisis. Passing through the lobby of the sanitorium, two Christian business men, sitting there in conversation, called us to them with the question, "Where were you at such a time?" naming the evening of the incident above mentioned. "Praying with a child of the Lord, who in a few moments will pass through a critical surgical operation," was the response. "I wonder if her financial needs are all met?" was the instant reply from one of them. Like a flash it came to us, "Our Father is working in answer to our asking." As the kind-hearted questioner kept pressing his inquiry, we replied: "Well, to tell the truth, her bills at the office are not even paid." Putting his hand in his pocket he drew forth a roll of notes and said, "Here are twenty-five dollars. Take it and use it for that purpose." Five dollars more were added to it, and, with the sum in our hand, we hastened to the ante-room of the surgical ward, and were given access to our friend. "See! Without a single human appeal, the Lord Himself has sent you thirty dollars toward the supply of your needs." Again her eyes filled with tears, but this time with tears of joy; and she said, tremulously, "How can I ever doubt Him again I" and passed into the dreaded operation room with a smile of joy upon her countenance.

It should be said here that she did not know the amount of her account at the office, nor did we. We had simply prayed God to supply her need, and this sum of thirty dollars had come. We now hastened to the office and asked for a transcript of Miss A.'s account. The clerk handed it to us. It was for twenty-nine dollars and seventy-six cents! We took it, and writing on the back of it: "My God shall supply all your need," put it in her letter box that it might be the first message which would greet her when she came back from the blessed swoon of painlessness which ether gives to all sufferers. She did come back and with marvelous rapidity. In four weeks she was entirely restored and starting for her distant home and the loved mother to whom God had given her back. But as we looked into her happy face and said good bye, we were saying it to a transformed woman – a woman who, as never before, knew the reality of prayer and the faithfulness of God in His deliverance from the darkest crisis of her life.

* * * *

"If we ask, God will do in our service."

Concerning those things that only God can do we naturally betake ourselves to prayer. For, knowing that we, ourselves, can not do them, we find our hope only in that asking which brings God's doing. But let us remember, too, that our own personal service, in the things which *we can do,* needs also that asking which will bring God's doing into it. Do we realize that everything we do needs to be saturated with the spirit of prayer that God may be the real doer, the real worker in the things which we are busily doing? Yet this is a mighty truth: "If ye ask, I will do" applies to your own service as well as your intercession for others.

Have you ever toyed with the key of a telegraph instrument while the circuit was closed? If so you have noted this fact: On that key you may write a complete message, from address to signature. Upon it every telegraph character may be perfectly formed; every condition of expert operating may be fulfilled. But it matters not how skilful an operator you are, so long as the electric circuit is closed, all your efforts are simply sounding brass and clattering platinum Not a single spark of electric life do you transmit; not a single message of good or ill, of bane or blessing, is conveyed to the waiting listener at the other end of the line. Why? Because the battery is not working. And all your working is effort without result, activity or power. But now you open the little brass lever which connects your key to the battery hidden beneath the table. Immediately every letter you form fills with life, every word you write flashes a living message into the mind and heart of the far-away receiver. Through your work, dead and mechanical in itself, the electric battery is now pouring forth its vital stream, flooding with life and power every deft motion of your flying fingers. The lesson is plain. It is in spiritual telegraphy as in material. If the battery is not working the message is mere clatter. WE may do, but if God is not doing through us, then all our doing is naught. If we work in our own fleshly strength we will but effect fleshly results only, for "Whatsoever is born of the flesh is flesh." God alone is spiritual life. God is the only begetter of life.

The supreme service for a believer is to be a transmitter of divine life. He is the channel between dead men and a life-giving God. Prayer-less, the channel is clogged and no life is linked to his touch upon men. Prayerful, the channel is wide open and God's life can flow unhindered through him to those so sorely needing it. "It is the Spirit that quickeneth," and if the believer is not, through prayer, in such an attitude that this same Spirit can work through him, his works are "dead works" and the life and power of God are absent from them.

It is a glorious privilege to stand as a messenger or minister between a life-giving God and dying men. But it is awful failure to be, through prayerlessness, so out of connection with that God that His life cannot flow through us to such souls in need of it. For eloquence is mere clamor, and rhetoric a supreme impertinence, when they thrust themselves forward as substitutes for the life of God flowing through the Spirit-filled man or woman, who through touch with Him by prayer and communion, offer Him an open channel for the forth-flowing of His quickening power to others.

From the chamber of prayer you come forth to men with the unction, the subtle power, the thrill of God's own life upon you, and as you touch them in speech, deed or prayer, "virtue goes forth from you," for then it is not you, but God that worketh in you. As you keep asking God keeps doing. When you grow prayerless, your deeds grow powerless. Lead no meeting without asking that God may be the real leader through you; speak no message without asking that He may speak through you; begin no work without asking that God may work through you. For

"If ye ask, I will do"

* * * *

If we ask, God will do in our impossibilities.

If we ask, God will do things which we ourselves cannot do. Here stands a heavy freight train upon a steep and difficult grade. A hundred stalwart men come forth and seek to move it. Putting their shoulders to the cars they tug and strain to the utmost limits of their strength, but they cannot stir the great train one inch. At last they give up the task in despair, as one hopelessly beyond their own power. And now comes along a little lad. He makes no attempt to move the train, for he knows it is hopeless. But he walks quickly to the head of the train, where a quiet man sits in the cab of the engine. Looking up into the face of the engineer, the lad says,

"Engineer, will you please move this train." the engineer turns around, lays hold of a little steel lever, gives it one pull, and behold the great train starts up the mountain under the power of the gigantic locomotive with perfect ease. What a hundred men had failed in with all their doing, one weak child had accomplished by his simple asking.

When Lazarus died, how little could the loved ones in the home at Bethany do for him. They could not bring back the flush of life to his pallid brow. They could not give strength and health to the loved one lying cold and still in death. But what they could not do, Christ could do for them, and when they sent for him the dead was raised at His simple word. There were five thousand hungry men on the green sward that day listening to His message. The disciples could not feed them. But Christ could. And when they asked He did. The disciples were helpless that night when the storm arose upon the sea. They toiled at the oars, but the night grew darker and the storm fiercer. They could do nothing to quell it. But when they called upon Him He did, and at His word of "Peace, be still," the tempest was stilled.

Think a moment of that unsaved loved one for whom all these years you have been doing. You have pleaded, argued and expostulated in vain. You have preached Christ; you have tried to live Christ; you have exhausted every device and means that love, faith or hope could conceive.

Now that all your doing has failed how wondrous it would be to bring into that life His doing through your asking.

What an unheard of privilege would you count it to have Jesus Christ Himself deal in person with a soul you loved! To have Jesus Christ work – not indeed in the body, but in the Spirit – in your home, your church, your community; to have Jesus Christ give secret messages to your lost loved ones; to have Jesus Christ speak, woo and win, as none else could; to have Jesus Christ with all His tact, wisdom, winsomeness, patience, gentleness, compassion, following on with unwearied zeal and tenderest love to bring back to God that soul for whom He had died. What a promise! and yet this is exactly what prayer will accomplish, for He explicitly says "If ye ask I will do."

Hear Him speak: "My child you know not how convict of sin, but I, who work as you pray, can bow down that soul in a very agony of conviction. You know not when to woo, and when to reprove, but I, who work as you ask, know just when to pour in the balm of love, and when to let fall the sharp quick blow of needed judgment. You cannot follow a soul in daily unbroken pursuit, for you are finite and must eat, rest, and sleep, but I who do as you ask, follow that soul day and night with sleepless vigilance, through every second of his existence, now comforting, now troubling; now giving darkness, now light; now sending prosperity, now adversity; now using the knife, now the healing balm; chastening, troubling, bereaving, blessing, tending, breaking, making, yea I can do all things needful to be done to bring that wanderer to himself and cause him to cry "I will arise and go unto my Father."

Even thus, if we ask, God will do things which we ourselves cannot do. Are there obstacles in your life which are insurmountable to you? But they are not so to God, if you but ask. Is there darkness veiling the pathway of life which seems to you impenetrable? But God will pierce the gloom if you but come to Him in believing prayer. Are there heart-breaking burdens which are too heavy for you to bear? God will bear them and in due time lift them, if you will but ask Him. Never be deterred from prayer by the difficulty of the thing to be done. Ask yourself only this one question: "Is it God's will to deliver me at this point?" If so, it matters not how hard the thing is from a human standpoint. God does not say "If ye ask, I will help you to do," but "If ye ask, I will do." That is, the answers to our prayers are the deeds of God. Therefore we should not be surprised if they bear the stamp of God's omnipotence. Is an omnipotent act any harder for an omnipotent God than a weak act for a weak human agent? Let us ever remember this: It is easy for God to do hard things. "Is there anything too hard for the Lord?" was the question the Holy Spirit put to Sarah's unfaith. And the answer comes back from that same Holy Spirit, "There is nothing too hard for Thee, O Lord." It is as easy for God to do a miracle, if He so wills, as it is for you and me to draw a breath, yea, a good deal easier. With God there are no such things as difficulties. Let us therefore bring the hard things, the insurmountable things, the impossible things to Him, and then things which we ourselves could not possibly do, He Himself says

"If ye ask I will do"

* * * *

If we ask God will do in our helplessness. What a message is this for God's children who, through years of pain and affliction as invalids and "shut-ins," have mourned because cut off from the active service in which others are busy for God. Beloved sufferers, be comforted. Blessed as is the ministry of doing, there is no higher, holier calling under heaven than that asking which calls forth God's doing in the lives of others. Your Master, Jesus Christ, through every second of His eternal, heavenly life, is pouring out His soul in unceasing asking ("He ever liveth to make intercession.") What an honor that God should call you to that same eternal ministry to which His great Son now unceasingly gives Himself! Covet no other if this be thine. To enter into a needy life with your own doing is indeed precious, but to have God enter it trough your asking, is it not greater by so much as God's doing is greater than thine?

One of the greatest spiritual writers of the age has said, "I am not sure but that God is not doing more through our praying than through our working." As you think of the doers in God's kingdom, as you contrast your own helplessness your heart grows heavy at the thought of how little you are accomplishing for Him and His kingdom. But, beloved, it is not more doers that are needed to-day, but more prayers. The church has a multitude who know how to work in their own power. But it has but few who know how to bring down God's power through prayer. The church is so busy doing its own work that it has no time to pray for God to work! So the only way God can get some of us to praying for His working is to lay us aside from our own. "If I were only well and strong," you say, "how much I could do for God." Yes, and if you were well and strong you would likely be like so many more strong ones – working away independently of God. But now, in your weakness, you are thrown upon God as the strong are not, and you may bring down such blessing into God's vineyard as none of the strong ever will.

Hear Him speak to you. "O child of mine, laid upon a bed of helplessness and suffering, cease to repine because thou canst not busy thyself with thine own doing, as others. For I tell thee that as in the silence of the night watches thou dost cry unto me for a lost world, I am doing what of my will thou art asking. Would'st thou not rather call forth mine omnipotent doing by thine asking, if to this I have called thee, than even to be busy with thine own doing? For if thou shalt ask (according to my will) I will do." And let your glad answer be, "Lord, I rejoice. Though, shut within these four walls, I cannot touch men, yet Thou, who hast promised to do for me, wilt touch and quicken them if I but ask. Though I am all the day weary and helpless, yet Thou, who hast promised to do for me, art in Thy doing tireless and omnipotent. Though I cannot raise a hand nor stir a foot, yet Thou, who hast promised to do if I ask, will move heaven and earth to bless those for whom I pray. Though my human asking must soon end with my passing away, yet Thy mighty doing called forth by my asking, will go on through all time, yea through eternity itself. Yea, Lord, since I can pray down Thy mighty doing into the lives I love, shall I longer mourn because I am shut out from my doing? What though I cannot do, if Thou, who dost work at my asking can do miracles? So, Lord, though I can do nothing, help me to remember with new joy and hope Thy blessed promise,

"If ye ask, I will do."

V. THE GREAT CONDITION.

"If we ask anything according to His will, He heareth us." I Jno. 5:14

* * * *

If answer is sure for all prayer that is according to His will, how eager we should be to learn that will if possible. But "we know not what we should pray for as we ought." Do we not rush into God's presence with our plans all prepared and importune Him to approve of them instead of waiting on Him to know His will for our life and then ask according to that will? Do we not try to win God over to yield to our desires instead of yielding to Him and praying according to His desires for us? We are cautious about doing things according to His will. Are we equally careful about asking things according to His will? We send up hosts of petitions to Him without the slightest confidence of answer, because we have not sought the "according to His will," which alone gives us confidence. Herein we are like children who, in capricious sport, launch their chip boats by the score upon the swift flowing river with no expectation of their return. Whereas we should be like thoughtful ship-owners sending out fewer crafts, but confidently looking for their rich-laden return because a definite cargo has been promised in the distant port to which they are sailing. There is an immature prayer life as surely as their is an immature Christian walk. In our earlier experience we make prayer a mere means of obtaining our own desires. In our later it becomes, as it should be, a mighty instrument for carrying out the will of God. Then we put up more petitions; now we get more answers. Then we sow more seed; now more of it comes up. The hound that hath a sure trail runs with confidence, while his doubting companion stands baying aloft in disappointed perplexity. The Christian that hath through the Spirit a keen scent (Isa. 11:3, Margin) to detect the will of God, prays with an assurance and power unknown to him who knows not what to pray for as he ought.

It is only as we ask according to the will of God that we can have this confidence or assurance in prayer.

For "This is the confidence that we have in Him, that if we ask anything according to His will He heareth us." If we are not asking in His will, this assurance of answer cannot be present.

Therefore seek so far as possible to know God's will concerning the object of your prayers.

Suppose you go to a man to borrow a sum of money. You know he is able to lend it. You know also that you sorely need it. But you do not know whether it will be convenient for him to give it; or whether he thinks you really need it or will to be able to repay it. In short you do not know his will in the matter. Therefore, while you have hope, yet you have no certainty or confidence that the money will be forthcoming. While you have all faith in him, yet you do not know his will, and therefore must continue in doubt and uncertainty as to the result until you hear from him. But now suppose you have a letter from him in which he states that he has heard you are in need and promises if you call upon a certain day he will pay you a certain sum. You now come to him with more than faith. You come with absolute, unquestioning confidence, that you will get the money desired. You do not need to inquire as to his will for that is already revealed in the promise made to you. You now simply ask according to that will perfectly assured that you will receive. Exactly thus is it in prayer. We desire something. Coming to God as to a loving father we ask. But if we are not certain that our wish is His will in the matter, we can only say "if it be thy will," and leave the matter with Him. We may be trustful, and hopeful, but we cannot be confident if not asking according to His will. For our trust rests in the person of God and cannot be disturbed by ignorance of His will at some point But our confidence of a certain specific answer to our prayer must rest in the fact that we are praying according to God's will, since we have no right to expect that He will give us that which is contrary to His will. Therefore when we pray in line with His will we are in the place of power. We wait quietly, trustfully, confidently. The thing asked for must come to pass, for He has willed ft and nothing can frustrate it.

How then shall we come to know His will in order that we may pray according to it, and so have Him do for us that which we ask?

There are three means by which we may know God's will, namely:

By *The Word.*
By Circumstances.
By The Spirit.

I. BY THE WORD.

Plainly, we may know His will first through His Word. For His Word is the revelation of His will for us and for the world, both now and hereafter. As we search for it, let us see clearly what His will is, and then definitely plead that will in prayer. Hence the value of knowing the promises of God in our prayer-life. When we find such a definite promise, it becomes the very base-stone of our confidence in prayer. We rest upon it with absolute certainty. We do not say, "if it be thy will," but "Lord, this is thy will clearly revealed, and praying according to that will, I know I shall be heard." Think, for instance, of the words, "My God shall supply all your need." The promise is clear, not that God will supply luxuries, but that He will supply His children's needs. There are things in life such as food, raiment, and the like, of Christ said, "Your heavenly Father knoweth that ye have need of these things." Therefore, when a child of God comes to his Father in prayer concerning these things, he is not to pray, "Father, if it be Thy will," but to plead, "Father, Thou hast clearly revealed that it is Thy loving will to supply all my needs, and therefore I pray according to that will with the greatest boldness and confidence, knowing that if I ask anything according to Thy will Thou wilt do it." Therefore, search the Word carefully for the explicit promises of God. Equipped with these, we have a supply of ammunition that never fails in out battles with the evil one. It was because Christ could say "it is written," that He thrust at Satan with such confidence and success.

But even as the very lighthouse which has oftenest guided a ship into the harbor would be the one which a foe would seek to blind, destroy, or misplace, if he wanted to lure that ship to destruction, so the very fact that the Word of God is what the Christian is depending upon for guidance, is what makes mis-quoted, mis-applied, or distorted Scripture the most dangerous instrument the adversary can use to mislead the believer as to the real will of God. It was this Word which Satan used when he tried to lead our Lord astray. And every error, or false doctrine, which men propagate, owes its dangerous influence to the misapplied Scripture which is cited in support of it. Therefore it behooves the believer to search the Word with greatest care lest the adversary may be using this subtlety to deceive him in this regard. *Let him be sure that the word which men quote in support of their doctrines is God's Word and not the opinion of men with regard to that Word.*

Be sure of the Translation. – The Word of God as we have it, being a translation from another language, needs to be searched for the new light that its newer translation may bring to us. Witness the passage in Acts 19: 3. In the Authorized Version it reads, "Have ye received the Holy Ghost since ye believed?" This has given rise to the insistent teaching by many that the Spirit of God is not received at regeneration, but at some stage subsequent to it because the Word says *"since* ye believed." But when we turn to the Revised Version we find this passage reading, "Did ye receive the Holy Ghost when ye believed?" which gives it an utterly different meaning, and shows that the Holy Spirit was expected to be

61

received at, and not after, regeneration. So in I Thess. 4:15, we read that the living in Christ shall not "prevent" the dead. This translation fills the verse with darkness and confusion, because the word "prevent" which now means to "hinder" meant, when the Bible was first translated, to "precede." Immediately that we substitute as in the Revision this word "precede" the meaning becomes perfectly clear, and utterly different from the King James translation. Many other passages might be cited to show the need of our being sure as to the translation of the Word.

Be sure also of the Context. – There is no misreading of the Word more common and none more fruitful of error than to read it without its context. Many, for example, quote I Jno. 1:7, "The blood of Jesus Christ His Son cleanseth us from all sin," as proving that by one definite act of faith the believer may be cleansed, by the blood of Christ, from the sinful nature within him. But mark the context, – "If we walk in the light, as He is in the light," the blood cleanseth, or keeps cleansing, etc. In other words the cleansing is a daily, continuous cleansing, conditioned on the believer's walking in Christ. But if he does not thus keep walking, the blood will not keep cleansing. Without the context the verse can be, and is, wrested to mean an instantaneous work of the blood of Christ through an act of faith. But with the context the verse refers to the continuous work of the blood of Christ through the daily walk of faith, to the abiding of the believer, not to his standing. The condition is not "If we believe," but "If we walk" The result is not "cleanseth" by an act, but "keeps cleansing," by a process, as the word means. To tear a passage from its needed context in this fashion, is like catching a single sentence from the words of a passer-by without knowing the subject matter whereof he speaks. The process is as unfair to the speaker as it is fatal to the truth. Again: –

Be sure of the Application. – Many texts of Scripture are true for the especial individuals to whom they were written, but do not have application to God's people at large. There is a vast mass of prophecy for example, which was written for the Jew, and has no application whatever to the Church, save for such general spiritual lessons as all may draw from it. There are promises to the Church on the other hand which are not applicable to Israel. Therefore, as we search the Word of God to know His will, it behooves us to ask, concerning any specific statement, "Does this apply to all, and therefore to me, or was it written to special persons or classes of persons only? Take for example the precious truth of the coming again of our Lord as prophesied in such passages as I Thess. 4:13-18. Many apply this to a coming at the death of the believer, arguing that Christ so comes at that time. The most casual study of the context can scarcely fail to show the glaringness of such a mis-application. Then too such a beautiful chapter as Isaiah 11, is "spiritualized" and made to refer to the glory of the Church in this Holy Ghost age, whereas a careful reading of it shows clearly and fully its reference to the restoration of Israel, and the conditions of peace and righteousness which dwell upon the earth in the Millennial reign of our Lord, and never until then. We vividly recall the case of a recruit in an army camo during the war with Spain who came to our tent in great trepidation of spirit because he was assured, from a chance reading of Romans 15:28, that he would surely be assigned to Spain before the war was finished. Scarcely less grotesque than this are the misapplications of God's Word made by many, by tongue and pen. The worst feature of errors of this sort is the serious injury to the faith of the person deceived. He pleads some promise of God from the Word, as he thinks, and then because God does not make it true in his life he loses faith in God and in the reality and power of prayer, whereas the failure to receive from God has been due purely to the fact that he has not been praying according to God's will, but according to his own false conception of it.

Be sure of your Inference. – Another common experience of misguidance in the truth of the Word is this. A speaker or writer quotes a text of Scripture and quotes it correctly. But straightway he proceeds to deduce an inference of his own from the text, and presently the reader, if not very careful, is accepting that human inference as the Word of God. Most of the absurd teachings of Christian Science find their lodgment and their power of beguilement from this cause. Its victims, all unconsciously to themselves, are accepting weak, absurd, illogical statements of men as the very Word of God itself, whereas they are only subtle human inferences inwoven with the text. Safeguarding ourselves then against these errors by the above simple precautions we shall find the Word of God a safe, and infallible guide for the revelation of His will in our prayer life.

Again, God reveals His will to His children

II. BY CIRCUMSTANCES.

A man's life may be so hedged by circumstances that they become a clear means of guidance to him upon points which the Word of God may not specifically touch. Thus the Word of God may call a man to go into all the world and preach the gospel. But to what part of the world that servant is to go, whether India, Africa, China or elsewhere, must be determined largely by circumstances outside of that Word. A man without a right arm would not be called by God into a work requiring the use of such. A man upon whom God had clearly laid the support of others who could not go into the foreign field could not go himself until God had changed those circumstances. God leads both by shutting doors of circumstance, and by opening them. Sometimes the clear closing or opening of the way by a circumstance becomes the chief sign we have of God's will in the matter at stake. The gifts which one possesses for Christian service, the joy he finds in doing it, the seal of success which God sets upon it may all be very definite circumstances to lead a man to the mind of God concerning his call to it. It must be noted, however, that circumstances alone are not usually the safe or the only means of guidance as to God's will. And the safe course here is always to

Confirm Circumstances by the Spirit of God.

That is, in all cases of any doubt as to God's will, wait upon God in prayer until assured in the Spirit that the course to which circumstances seem to point is the one to be taken. In other words, there is sometimes a speciousness, a plausibleness in circumstances which may lead us astray unless tested and confirmed by the Spirit of God. Who of us has not had the experience of having all things seem to point in a certain direction, to a certain course of action, yet there has been a slight hesitancy of spirit, a lack of perfect liberty to so act. We delayed. And then as we waited in prayer the circumstances changed, or lost their weight with us, and we came to see clearly that we would have been mistaken in following them. This plausibleness of circumstances is well illustrated in the ninth chapter of Joshua. The Gibeonites were a part of the old inhabitants of the promised land who were to be destroyed, or driven forth by Joshua and the Israelites. Knowing the fate which would meet them if they were recognized as dwellers in the land, they came to Joshua feigning to be ambassadors from a distant country, and showing in proof thereof their bread, dry, musty and moldy from their pretended long and weary journey. Joshua and the Israelites were deceived by a circumstance the dry and musty bread. In the graphic language of the text (Josh. 9:14) *"They received the men by reason of their victuals* (margin) *and asked not counsel at the mouth of the Lord."* The inference is plain that if they had waited upon the Lord and taken counsel of Him He would have unmasked the guile of the Gibeonites and shown Joshua that the circumstances were false and deceptive. Even so Satan is ever ready to mislead God's children by all sorts of trickery and will bait his traps with any device where-with he may ensnare them. The only safe course for us is always to "take counsel at the mouth of the Lord," and have Him confirm for a certainty all that is doubtful or even plausible in circumstances.

III. BY THE SPIRIT.

We may know the will of God also through the Spirit of God. For there are many emergencies in our lives in which neither the Word of God nor Circumstances can convey to us the mind of God, and unless there is a guidance by the Spirit of God His children must walk in darkness. The Word of God, for example, may call us to prayer for the sick, but there is nothing in that Word, nor in circumstances, which reveals to us whether it is, or is not, the will of God to raise up or to take to Himself the one for whom we may pray. And it is only as we wait upon God in prayer that we can receive, by the Spirit of God, the assurance of His will to heal or to take. The Word of God bids us to go forth into all the world and preach the gospel to every creature. But there is nothing in that Word which tells us into what particular part of the world a man so called is to go, and with nothing particular in the circatnstances to guide he may be thrown entirely upon the leading of the Spirit of God for light. Indeed there are hundreds of details in our lives in which we need the guidance of God to keep ns from going astray, and in which being guided directly neither by the Word nor Circumstances, the Spirit becomes the supreme, final and only revealer of God's will in the matter at issue. And why should it be thought impossible for the God who is a Spirit to guide those who have that same Spirit within them as a gift from Him? Yea, it is by the Spirit of God that the things of

God are revealed. And does not our denial, or skepticism as to the guidance of the Spirit rather prove our lack of perception than His lack of guidance? The fact that no voice conies to us over a telephone does not prove that there is no such voice. It may only mean that we have not heard it. That we do not hear the voice of the Spirit does not prove the silence of God, but only die dullness of our spiritual hearing. It is not that God is mute, but that we are deaf. Let us not deny the fact of the Spirit's inner voice to the soul merely because we are too fleshly to hear it. The Word of God clearly proves that He spoke to men by the voice of His Spirit. Of Paul and Silas it is said, Acts 16: 7, that they assayed to go into Bithynia but *"the Spirit suffered them not."* Of Philip that same word says that the Spirit said to Philip "Go near, and join thyself to this chariot." (Acts 8:29.) So we are told that Agabus spoke to Paul *"by the Spirit."*

Acts 21:11. As the disciples at Antioch fasted and prayed we are told that "The Holy Ghost said, 'Separate me Barnabas and Saul for the work whereunto I have called them.'" (Acts 13. 2.) Likewise does God speak by His Spirit to His children in these days.

There are three lessons we need to learn concerning the revelation of God's will through the Spirit. These are:

WILL.

"If any man will to do His will he shall know." To know the will of God we must will the will of God. Self-will is the surest and densest veil which hangs between us and the knowledge of God's will. To approach God in the spirit of self-will is like the plunge of a railroad train into a great tunnel – darkness and gloom are the sure result. It is through the heart, rather than through the head, that we discern the will of God, and rebellion or failure of submission in the heart means darkness upon the path. If we ask ourselves "Am I just as willing to have God refuse this petition of mine if it be His will, as to grant it?" we will find a sure test for unmasking self-will. And we will be amazed, as we apply this test, to discover how much of our prayer life is an effort to win God over to assent to, and carry out, our own will rather than an asking according to His will. To come to God then in the spirit of absolute submission to His will is a supreme essential to the knowing that will.

WAIT.

Haste is the parent of nine-tenths of our mistakes concerning the will of God. The man who hurries has many mis-steps to wearily retrace, where the man who waits has but few. Waiting on God is a kind of spiritual filter. The sediment of darkness and error precipitates for the man who waits, and the clear and luminous truth remains. Do not allow yourself to be driven to inconsiderate decisions under any pretext of haste. When you are in doubt you have a sure call to wait. It is astonishing how the mist will clear away and the light shine forth for the man who waits. The spirit of haste, on the other hand, is born of the flesh and its results cannot fail to be of the same.

WALK.

God is a Spirit. If we would receive the messages of the Spirit we must learn to walk in the Spirit.

Suppose from a loved one who has gone before a promise came that sometime to-morrow a Message would come to you from that other land. Suppose, too, that since that message was to be from a spiritual being you yourself must needs be walking in the Spirit if you would hear it. When to-morrow dawned how careful would you be lest you miss it. How careful about waiting on God; how careful to have your ear attuned to the coming tidings; how guarded lest the clamor and boisterousness of every-day life might dull your spiritual hearing. How much time would you spend in quietness in the chamber of prayer, waiting and listening in the silence. How earnestly would you seek to be in the Spirit when that message came from your loved one on the other shore, so that you might receive, hear and know it. Just this should be our continual attitude toward God. We should strive just as earnestly to be in the Spirit to hear God's messages to us as we would be to receive the message of an absent loved one, if such a thing were possible.

Neither let us lose heart if we are slow about learning how thus to so walk in the Spirit that we may recognize the inner voice when He speaks to us. For this selfsame thing is the highest test of the closeness of our walk with God. We can afford to yield a costly tribute of time and patience here in return for so precious a blessing. More than a century ago godly Pastor Blumhardt was wondrously used of God in prayer for the sick. His power in this ministry depended, as does all power in prayer, upon praying according to the will of God. He testified that at the first when he began this ministry of intercession, he would spend many hours in prayer before he could ascertain the will of God as to the afflicted one. But after about two years he came to be so familiar with the inner voice of God that often he would scarcely have lifted his heart to God in communion ere the mind of God in the matter was clearly revealed to him. With us, even as with him, God is willing if we are but patient, prayerful, and trustful. Here, as elsewhere, the Lord will give us the desire of our heart, and in kind, if not in degree, shall it be true of us, His own children, that "The Father loveth the Son and showeth him all things which He Himself doeth,"

VI. THE PRACTICE OE PRAYER.

"ASR" – Matt. 7:7

* * * *

The way to get a thing which is purchasable is to pay for it. The way to get a thing which is to be earned is to work for it. The way to get a thing which is to be given is to ask for it. The Christian in receiving from God has neither to pay nor to earn. What he gets from God comes by gift, and the way to receive it is simply to ask. In Matthew 7:7, God says, "Ask and ye shall receive, In Matthew 7: II, "How much more shall your Father which is in heaven give good things to them that ask him." In John 14: II, "Whatsoever ye shall ask in my name." In John 14:14, "If ye ask I will do." Since then the definite blessing in prayer comes from our simple asking, the first great lesson is: –

1. Begin to Ask. – When we come to a place of crisis or stress in our life we betake ourselves to everything but this. We worry, we fret, we brood, but we do not ask. But God does not say "If ye chafe, or scheme, or plan I will do, but if ye ask I will do." Does some one say here: "I do not know how to ask. I do not understand the mysteries of God's will. I do not know how to live this prayer life" The answer is simple.

The way to learn to do is to begin to do. This is true of all effort. It is also true of prayer. The trouble is not that we do not know how to ask, but that we are not asking. God can help the man who can not pray. The Holy Spirit

72

will teach him. But God cannot help the man who will not pray, for he gives God no chance. God does not expect us to know all the secrets of prayer before we enter into the school of prayer. He asks us to begin: to take our seat on the primary bench: to learn first the A, B, C, of this life. And then as we go on praying, we keep on learning. The responsibility of teaching to pray is with God. But the responsibility of praying is with us. It is not our ignorance of the prayer life, but our woful neglect of it that most grieves the heart of God.

2. *Be instant in Asking.* – That is, ask before you do anything else. Men say here, "God helps those who help themselves. Do the best you can and when you can do no more call on God for help." This sounds wise, but it is a specious wisdom. We ourselves have no power to meet the wiles of Satan, and if we essay to do so alone, we will be overpowered. Therefore go first to God in prayer. Go to Him first that you may have His guidance. Go to Him first that you may have light from His Word. Go to Him first that you may be strengthened by His Spirit. Go to Him first that you may be kept from mistakes, the correction of which may take many long and weary days. A beautiful example of so going first to God in prayer is found in the second chapter of Nehemiah. Nemehiah's heart was burdened for the rebuilding of his beloved city, for the restoration of his people. He came into the presence of the king with a sad countenance. The king seeing it said, "Why art thou sad of countenance to-day? For what dost thou make request?" And Nehemiah answered, and said, "If it please the king that thou would send me unto the city of my fathers that I may build it." But note that in the

brief instant which elapsed between the question of the king and the answer of Nehemiah occurs this remarkable sentence, "So I prayed to the God of Heaven" Nehemiah in answering the question of the king, did not dare trust his own wisdom, but even in the few seconds of time that were his he lifted up his heart to God in prayer and cried to God for wisdom in his reply. Some one has called this "ejaculatory prayer," from the Latin word, "jaculum," meaning a javelin or dart. That is, Nehemiah sent up, as it were, a little arrow of prayer to God for help. There is a precious lesson for us in this. A great crisis comes into our life: a great need is present there. We do not have time to go apart into our closet and commune with God, for the emergency is too sudden. But we can do as Nehemiah did. We can be one of God's "Minute men" in prayer. Just where we are, on the street, in the place of business, in the very midst; of the rush and pressure of daily affairs, we can send up one of these little arrows of prayer: – "Lord help me; Lord guide me; Lord give me wisdom in this crisis." This habit of being in instant, momentary prayer-touch with God in the busy rush of life is as precious in its way as the longer periods of communion which come to us in the quiet and retirement of the closet.

3. Keep on Asking. – "Pray without ceasing," says the apostle in 1 Thess. 5:17. Just what does the Spirit mean here? Hardly that we should spend every moment of our lives in actual, audible prayer. But probably, first, that we should constantly be in an attitude of prayer to God amid all the circumstances of life: that the atmosphere of our life should be one of prayerfulness. Added to this is also the thought that we are to pray, as it were, "without *ceasings*" that is, without great gaps and interruptions in our prayer life. We know the evil of constant breaks, and interruptions in our daily tasks. The lad who is in school one week and stays away the next will never become a scholar. The musician who is faithful to his practice for a time, and then wholly neglectful of it, will never become master of his art. So if we pray to-day and forget to pray to-morrow; if we cry to God this week and are silent next, our prayer life will suffer in the same way. We pray with ceasings, with interruptions, and we lose power in so doing. God wants us to pray without cessations, without gaps and intervals in our intercession. "Pray without ceasing" then is a warning against fitfulness, and remittingness in prayer. It is a call to habitual, rather than to never-ceasing prayer. It is the daily, regular, habitual holding on to God that brings things to pass in the kingdom of prayers. To such a petitioner there comes sense of grip; a feeling that he is prevailing: a consciousness of effectiveness in prayer which is not present where inconstancy and remittingness mar the prayer life. If we stay our lips and hearts from the daily practice of prayer we shall as surely fail of success, as the apprentice who ofttimes slacks his hand from the cunning of his trade will fall short of becoming a master-workman therein.

Again we are not only to pray without ceasing hut also to pray without fainting. "And He spake a parable unto them, that men ought always to pray and not to faint." (Luke 18: 1) The first is a warning against fitfulness in prayer, the second against lack of perseverance therein. For this, like that, ensnares many. No temptation in the life of intercession is more common than this of failure

75

to persevere. We begin to pray for a certain thing; we put up our petitions for a day, a week, a month, and then, receiving, as yet, no definite answer, straightway we faint, and cease altogether from prayer concerning it. This is a deadly fault. It is simply the snare of many beginnings with no completions. It is ruinous in all spheres of life. The man who forms the habit of beginning without finishing has simply formed the habit of failure. The man who begins to pray about a thing and does not pray it through to a successful issue of answer has formed the same habit in prayer. As in everything else so it is in prayer. To faint is to fail. Then defeat begets disheartenment, and unfaith in the reality of prayer, which is fatal to all success. It were better to put up fewer prayers and get more answers than to have on hand a host of unfinished petitions, with all the spiritual de-moralization that flows therefrom.

More than a half century ago George Muller that prince of intercessors with God, began to pray for a group of five personal friends. After five years one of them came to Christ. In ten years two more of them found peace in the same Saviour. He prayed on, for twenty-five years, and the fourth man was saved. For the fifth he prayed until the time of his death, and this friend too came to Christ a few months afterward. For this latter friend Mr. Muller had prayed almost fifty-two years! When we behold such perseverance in prayer as this we realize that we have scarcely touched the fringe of real importunity in our own intercessions for others.

But some one says here: "How long shall we pray? Do we not come to a place where we may cease from our petitions and rest the matter in God's hands? There is but one answer. – Pray until the thing you pray for has actually been granted, or until you have the assurance in your heart that it will be. Only at one of these two places dare we stay our importunity. For prayer is not only a calling upon God, but also a conflict with Satan. And inasmuch as God is using our intercession as a mighty factor of victory in that conflict, He alone, and not we, must decide when we dare cease from our petitioning. So we dare not stay our prayer until the answer itself has come, or until we receive the assurance that it will come. In the first cases we stop because we see. In the other we stop because we believe. And the faith of our heart is just as sure as the sight of our eyes, for it is faith from, yea the faith OF God, within us. More and more as we live the prayer life shall we come to experience and recognize this God-given assurance, and know, when to rest quietly in it, or when to continue our petitioning until we receive it.

4. *Ask in ALL Things.* – "Be anxious in nothing but in everything by prayer," etc. (Phil. 4:6). We go to God in prayer when some great need or crisis comes into our life, but in the little things which fill up those lives we forget to pray. But God wants us to be prayerful in all things. And the reason is clear. For prayer brings the peace of God. Hence when we bring a worriment or anxiety to God we shift the burden of it from ourselves to God, and this brings us peace. Now if we only bring to God, and lay upon God in prayer, the great burdens of life, then we have peace only concerning these. But the most of our life is made up of little things, of everyday happenings, of a multitude of seeming trifles.

Wherefore so far as we keep these out of our prayers, we keep peace out from our lives. And this is why our peace is fitful in stead of perfect. It is because our prayer life is only partial instead of all-inclusive. If we prayed about all things we would have peace about all things. Wherever prayer is missing peace is absent. Stonewall Jackson, speaking of this truth, said: "When I write a letter I ask God to go with it. When I speak a word I ask Him to bless it. When I do anything for Him I ask His presence in it. In all things I try to come to Him in prayer." Even thus would God have all His children live the life of prayer.

5. Ask and ye shall know God. – Manasseh, wandering from God, lost his throne, and was carried away captive. In his distress he cried unto the Lord, and the Lord heard, and restored him. "Then Manasseh knew that the Lord He was God (2 Chron. 33:13). An answer to prayer is a personal introduction to God. To see the artist paint before your eyes until the canvass glows with beauty makes painting very real. To see the sculptor chisel and carve a rare statue while you watch makes sculpture very real. To cry to God in trouble, and to see the very thing you asked for come into your life exactly as you asked for it, makes the Lord wondrously real. It was when Manasseh cried and the Lord heard that then Manasseh knew God as never before. It is like hearing the voice, touching the hand and looking into the eyes of a friend whom you before only knew by reputation. "Hereby shall ye know that the living God is among you " said Joshua to the Israelites (Josh. 3:10.) That is the mighty works which God would do for them would make God real and tangible to them. Perhaps you

are a student, a worker at the desk. Some day you go away leaving your table in confusion and disarray. When you return you find it in perfect order. Your books are neatly piled; your scattered papers are orderly arranged; every article has found its proper place; a rose, or sprig of heliotrope adds beauty and fragrance to it all. You recognize the presence and thoughtfulness of a loved one. You see and know the hand by these traces of its ministry. Thus is it in prayer. To the man who cries to God in prayer the doing of God which comes in reply to that asking makes God so real and practical in his life that you cannot possibly convince him these things are chance, or accident, or anything else than the personal presence of his Lord working mighty works and deeds in his own life. He knows God as the prayerless man can never know Him, because he thus sees His direct and loving touch upon every interest of his life.

6. Ask – *and your joy shall be Full.* – There are many kinds of joy pictured in God's Word. There is the joy of salvation. "Rejoice not in this, but rejoice that your names are written in heaven," said Christ to the seventy. (Luke 10:20.) There is the joy of seeing a soul brought to Christ, a sight which fills the hearts of even the angels of heaven as they behold. (Luke 15:7.) There is the joy of being wholly yielded up to God to do His Will, which is the very joy of Christ himself in us, and which makes our to be full. (John 15:11.) Of like preciousness is the joy of answered prayer. "Ask and ye shall receive that your joy may be full," says our Lord. (John 16:24.) Very wondrous indeed is the gladness which fills our hearts when a great answer to prayer

comes into our life. To pray amid darkness, and have God send great light: to pray in the face of a great barrier, and see God tear it down before our very eyes: to cry amid a dire need and have God swiftly and wondrously supply it – what joy floods the heart at the moment God sends such answers! The very joy of heaven itself enters into our life in such an experience. It is born of God, and no human joy can match it. What a constant stream of joy keeps flowing through the life of a child because of the gifts which his father gives at his asking. Would not this same river of joy burst forth in the lives of many of God's children who, now joyless and unhappy, if they only knew this secret of the joy of answered prayer and practiced it?

7. Ask – because there is a giving by God which comes only from our asking. –   Prayer is a power. Through prayer God does things which would not otherwise be done. When He says – "If ye ask, I will do." He very clearly hints that if we do not ask there will be some lack of His doing. This is a great mystery but it is also a great fact. When Hezekiah, in distress, prayed to God for deliverance from the Assyrian host, and God sent His angel who smote one hundred and eighty-five thousand of them, the reason for that victory was stated in these words – "Thus saith the Lord (to Hezekiah), Whereas thou hast prayed to me." The deliverance came because he had prayed. (Isa.37:21.) Christ, too, speaking of the friend who came at midnight for bread, said, "Though he will not rise and give him because he is his friend, yet because of his importunity he will rise and give him as many as he needeth." (Luke 11:8.) Christ here clearly teaches that some things which God

80

does not give simply from the fact of being a God of grace, and because He is "our friend," He does give because of our importunity." God indeed gives many things simply because He is God, and a God of grace. He sends His rain on the just and the unjust. He has general blessings which He pours out whether we pray or not. But there are great and special bounties which He holds in reserve for those who pray, which he bestows because of our importunity. It is like this. Here are the heavens overarching us. They are always full of the moisture which is ready to descend in the form of rain. That rain is always, as it were, hanging over the heads of the children of men. But it does not descend in the form of rain until a cool current of air meets the moisture laden clouds condenses them into showers at that particular point. So these special gifts of are, as it were, His clouds hung over us big promise waiting for our stream of prayer to rise and condense them into showers of blessing, but if we pray not they float by leaving us unvisited unrefreshed. We have a beautiful illustration of this truth in Samson's life (Judges 15:18, 19). Samson had just won a great victory in the slaughter of a thousand of his enemies. He finds himself weary, and sore athirst. God looks down upon him and sees his condition but there is no deliverance recorded until Samson "called on the Lord." Then God's hand clave the earth and the living water gushed forth to revive and save the earnest petitioner. Wherefore Samson names the place "Enhakkore," that is: "The well of him that cried." "In that name he clearly testifies that the thing which most impressed him in this wonderful deliverance was that it was given when he cried. It was when he became a crier that God opened the well. And as the years rolled by and men quenched their thirst at the living spring its name was a constant reminder that God had opened it because some one had cried to Him."

How true this is in our lives! We come into some place of stress in life. The gloom is thick; the burden is heavy; the voice of hope is faint; the vision of faith is dimmed. While we are sore athirst God is waiting – waiting for our cry to Him. The very ground beneath our feet is throbbing with the pulse of the thirst-slaking fountain that is ready to spurt forth when we cry. But if we do not cry we have no well, for it is "the well of him that cries." Sometimes men shoot an oil well with a cartridge that spurts the fluid into the air by its force. So prayer is God's well opener. When we cry, the earth cleaves and the fountain bursts forth. Prayer is the passage-way from spiritual thirst to spiritual refreshing. "He was sore athirst – he called – and his spirit came again " It is the bridge that bears us from distress to deliverance: – "In my distress – I cried – and He delivered " Some know only the thirst, only the distress, because they use not the way out of both – the cry. God does not mean us to live in a permanent state of need or a permanent condition of distress, but out of the need and out of the distress to cry and have a well opened. One man says, pointing to the past "Here came a great affliction to me: – here a great temptation – here a grevious sorrow – here a serious loss. My life has been a constant experience of distress and need." Another says "True, I have been through the same tribulations. But see: – Here God opened for me a cooling well – here a sparkling fountain – here a bubbling spring – here a refreshing stream. Life sad for you because you know only its need – joyous for me because I know also the deliverance: – "for He shall deliver the needy when he crieth" Who is there, buffeted, dispirited, weary death, who has not cried unto Him in their distress and, in the quiet inflow of piece comfort, and rest, been as conscious that opened a stream of refreshing in their souls though their ears heard its musical flow, their parched lips tasted its sweet running waters.

What a searching word, to the same effect is that of the Holy Spirit in James 4:2, "Ye have not, because ye ask not" If you do not pray some laborer will not go forth into the harvest field; if you do not pray some darkened soul in China or Africa may not receive the Gospel of Jesus Christ; if you do not pray father, or sister, or loved friend may not be convicted of sin; if you do not pray some door that God would have opened may remain closed forever; if you do not pray some barrier may stand till Jesus comes that God might have hurled down if you had prayed. If you do not pray only eternity will reveal what God has lost and what you have lost and what the universe has lost because of your failure in asking.

Child of God, to-day there are obstacles in your life which seem to doom you to utter failure of God's highest purpose for you. You have planned, worried, toiled and failed. Despair is beginning to settle down upon you, and hope is fading away from your life, for all your doing has been thwarted. Try now the asking which brings His doing. Begin to live the prayer life. Ask, ask, ASK, and then out of all the failure of your doing look unto Hun who says "If ye ask, I will do." Pray – and He will soften hearts which all your doing could never touch; – and He will heal that cruel estrangement which is slowly crushing you; pray – and He will meet your needs, both temporal and spiritual; pray – and He will weave all the tangled threads of your life which seem beyond hope of disentanglement into the single golden strand of His great purpose for you; pray – and unto your life, fresh from the failure and disappointment of your doing, He will bring miracles of His doing which will some glad day fill your lips with songs of praise; pray – and He will work changes unthought of, and bring about providences undreamed of; pray – and He will overturn and overturn, until darkness changes to light, bondage to liberty, bridgeless chasms to safe highways, granite walls to webs of gossamer, because a miracle working God has fulfilled His premise

"If ye ask, I WILL DO."

VII. PRAYER AND HEALING.

"And the prayer of Faith shall save the sick." – Jas. 5:15.

* * * *

The truth concerning this important phase of prayer may be best considered under four heads, namely:

Is God *able* to heal?
Does God *ever* heal?
Does God *always* heal?
Does God *use means* in healing?

Is God able to heal?

We need not tarry here. There can be but one answer. The omnipotent God who made the body can just as easily heal it, if it be His will. There is no limit to His power, and to any child of His who believes in the omnipotence of God, there can be no difference of view here. Passing on then:

* * * *

Does God ever heal?

Here, too, there will be but little divergence of view. The Word of God plainly records the exercise of God's power in the healing of the sick. And not only was this true in the time of our Lord upon earth, but also even in all the centuries which have elapsed since He left it. There are too many authentic cases of the God's healing power in these latter days for any fair-minded man to deny the fact that He does still so exercise that power. But we approach a much more important and mooted question in the next point to be considered, and that is:

* * * *

Is it always the will of God to heal?

There is a large class of God's children who answer this question by an emphatic affirmative. They earnestly contend that it is the will of God to heal all sickness; that it is only our unbelief, our failure of appropriating faith, which keeps us from being healed in case of sickness, and that all who will really trust the Lord for healing and claim the same in Him, shall realize it in fact. This is one of the most important and vital teachings upon the whole theme and as it reaches the heart of the whole matter, the arguments of its advocates are worthy our most careful and prayerful attention. And first they claim that:

Healing is in the Atonement. – This is true in that every spiritual deliverance comes to us from the atonement. But it must be remembered that the atonement of Christ covers the Millennial age to come as well as this age in which we now live. And it does not follow that because the children of God are to be delivered from all disease and sickness that deliverance is for now instead of hereafter when "the inhabitants of Jerusalem," (that is, the dwellers in the Millennial age,) "shall no longer say 'I am sick.' " For it is clear that there are many blessings in the atonement, the fullness of time for the enjoyment of which has not yet arrived. Thus

86

deliverance from death is covered by the atonement of Christ. Yet it is not ours in this age, but in an age yet to come after the coming of our Lord. So too it is argued that Christ was made a curse for us and that we are therefore made free from all the curse of the law, and that under this is included sickness. But that we are not made free now from all the curse of the law is clear in that the curse upon the earth is clearly not removed until our Lord comes, and in Rom. 8:19-23 we see the whole creation groaning under this bondage and looking forward to another age for deliverance from its thralldom. Thus we see plainly that we cannot claim in this age all that is included under the atonement of Christ, and therefore cannot claim universal exemption from sickness on the ground that it is in the atonement of our Lord.

Sickness is of Satan, it is furthermore said, and therefore it must be the will of God to take it away. But in answer to this it may be said that there are many things which are of Satan, which God yet permits to exist until His time for their removal has come. Thus, as seen above, death is of Satan, yet God permits it for the present. Sorrow and suffering are of Satan, yet God suffers them for the present. Temptation is surely of Satan, yet God permits His children to be so assailed. So sickness may be an assault of the adversary upon our bodies, yet God permit it. God clearly permitted Satan to attack His servant Job. So too Paul's thorn in the flesh is clearly declared to have been "a messenger of Satan," yet God did not remove it. That it is not always God's will to heal seems clear:

By the Experience of His children. – After all is it not a fact of every-day observation that God does use physical affliction for the chastening and purification of His children, and that He suffers it to remain until He has accomplished His purpose of love and child-training with them. Surely this is the case in the lives of myriads of His godliest saints. Who is there of us who has not seen a strong, perhaps rebellious, life go into the crucible of affliction of all kinds, bodily included, and come forth strengthened and purified as no other dealing of God seemed hitherto able to accomplish. We recall the case of one of the most devoted and successful workers in the Lord's vineyard. For sixteen years she lay a helpless invalid, suffering keenly much of the time. At the end of all these long and weary years she awoke one midnight to the consciousness that she had never been wholly submitted to the will of God in her illness; that deep in her heart there had always been a root of bitterness, a spirit of rebellion that God should permit her thus to suffer. Then and there, with the vision of her rebellious will vividly before her, she yielded that will wholly and unconditionally to her Father in heaven, to patiently bear not only what He might send, but also all that He might permit to come into her life in the way of bodily affliction. She was as she expressed it, just as willing to lie there a thousand years, if it were God's will, or to be raised up to health if that were His will. Within a week she was marvelously, yea miraculously, healed by the power of God. All those years God had permitted her to stay under this bodily affliction to bring her into that place of absolute submission to His will, without which He never could have used her for the glorious work to which he was calling her. And do we not see

Him permitting others of His own thus to be afflicted not only for years, but for a whole lifetime, without the ensuing healing which came in this case? And as we mark the Christ-like patience, gentleness, and long-suffering which are wrought out in these lives in the chamber of affliction, must we not confess that for some reason God is suffering it to be thus? And dare we assert that the only reason such godly souls are not healed of their diseases is because they do not have faith in God? Such an inference is incredible to those who know the saintliness of many such lives. In the eleventh chapter of Hebrews we have a striking lesson along this line of truth. There we are told of some who "obtained promises, stopped the mouths of lions, quenched the violence of fire, escaped the edge of the "word," and in general, received mighty deliverance at the hand. ohf their God. But we are also told that "others were tortured, had trial of cruel mockings and scourgings, were stoned, were sawn asunder, were tempted, were slain with the sword; they wandered about in sheepskins and goatskins; being destitute, afflicted, tormented." What was the difference in these two classes? Were those who escaped delivered because they had faith in God, while the others were not delivered through lack of the same? Surely not. For we are distinctly told that they "all obtained a good report through faith" They all had exactly the same faith in God. That is, the "others" who were afflicted, destitute, and tormented were so not because of lack of faith in God, but because, in His inscrutable wisdom, God's will for them was different than for those who were delivered from the same perils and persecutions. Do we not often see God acting in precisely the same manner with those diseased and afflicted in body? Some He heals marvelously, miraculously. Others, for some cause best known to Himself, He permits to stay in the place of infirmity and affliction. It seems clear that it is not because these lack faith to be healed, if God will, but that it is not His will to heal.

We see again that it is not always God's will to heal:

Because of the silence of God's Word. – If, as many claim, it is the will of God that all should be healed, and those who fail of this do so through lack of faith in Him, then it seems strange that so wondrous and important truth as this should not be very clearly taught in the Word of God, and especially in the epistles, in which God gives special light and teaching for His church. And yet all through these epistles there is a notable and significant silence concerning any such teaching. True there are such passages in the Gospels, as Matt. 8:16, 17, in which we are told: "He healed all that were sick, that it might be fulfilled which was spoken by Esaias the prophet, saying, Himself took our infirmities, and bare our sicknesses." Yet this seems to be a foreshadowing of the time to come when all sickness and infirmity shall be taken away rather than for the present period in which we live. For Paul, we are told in 2 Tim. 4:20, left Trophimus at Miletum with one of these very "sicknesses"; and Paul himself continued to bear one of these self-same "infirmities" which was certainly not taken away in his case. 2. Cor. 12:7-9. If the deliverance from sickness and infirmities is so sweeping as is claimed, why should these and others be left under their power? But while the same epistles are so significantly silent as to the will of God to heal all sickness, they do set forth clearly and simply what God's own mind is upon this subject when they say in James 5:15, –

"The prayer of faith shall heal the sick"

What is taught here? Clearly, that sickness comes under the sphere of prayer. We are to come to God in prayer in sickness exactly as we comee to Him in prayer concerning anything else in our lives. Therefore being brought by God into the sphere of prayer it is subject to precisely the same conditions and the same great laws of prayer as anything else that falls within its domain. And one of the supreme and unchangeable laws of prayer is that only when we are praying according to God's will can we expect Him to hear and grant our petition. And that brings us to note the next point in the teaching of this passage in James, to wit, that: –

The prayer of faith shall save the sick. In other words the mere bringing the sick to God in prayer does not insure their healing. The mere praying to God and claiming healing does not bring that healing. There must be a certain kind of prayer, and only that kind of prayer, which is here called the prayer of faith, can insure the healing by the Lord of the one prayed for; only then "the Lord shall raise him up." It becomes then of supreme importance to answer aright the question "What is the Prayer of Faith?"

Note first that the faith of the prayer of faith, the only kind that brings healing, is not a forced faith. It is not that kind of faith which says, "If I ask for healing, all I have to do is to believe I am healed, and I shall be." Such a faith is spurious and man-made. It is not true that "whatever we ask of God we would get if we only had faith enough," as we sometimes put it. Such a conception of prayer is crude in the extreme. *All true faith rests not upon its own daring and rashness, but upon the revealed will of God.* We have no right to trust God for that which is not His will for us. The same Christ who trusted Him in the hunger of the wilderness did not dare to trust Him to keep Him in hurling Himself from the pinnacle of the temple – a thing which was not according to His will. God was just as able to do the latter as the former, but it was not His will. So that is not great faith which, without seeking to know His will, sets hard, rash things for God to do, and calls on Him to work up to them. But that is great faith which, waiting on God to know His will, when that will is once seen, rests without a quiver upon His eternal promise as sure that the prayer has been heard as though the thing prayed for were already in hand. "This is the confidence that we have in Him that if we ask anything according to His will he heareth us * * and we know that we have the petitions that we desired of Him." God does not expect us to believe except upon evidence from Him. He gives us that: evidence, as we saw in the preceding chapter, either through His Word, Providences, or inner witness of His Spirit. If, as we have seen, we have no revelation in His Word of universal healing, and none in His providences, then we have no right to believe save upon the one remaining evidence, namely the revelation of God to us by the inner witness of the Spirit. *The Prayer of Faith, then, is the prayer in which God Himself gives the petitioner an inward assurance by His Spirit that the thing he prays for is according to God's will and* *has been granted.* The prayer of faith can thus only be prayed in that which is according to God's will. If the petition is not according to His will God withholds this assurance. The absence of this assurance therefore is proof that it is not the will of God to heal the sickness concerning which we pray – unless indeed such lack of assurance is due not to God's unreadiness to give but our failure to spiritually discern the same through our unfamiliarity with the inward witness of God in prayer. But, barring this, we must have this confidence and assurance born of the Spirit of God, and not of our own imaginings, as the evidence that God has answered our prayer for the sick. No other prayer than this prayer of faith heals the sick, and if we do not have it we cannot claim the healing of which it is the only divine witness.

Our claims to healing if not thus founded may be only counterfeit, born of our own presumption and wilfullness instead of the inward witness of God by which "we know that we have the petition we have asked for." The general faith that God will heal because He is able to heal; or because He has healed others, or us at other times; or because Jesus Christ is "the same yesterday, to-day, and forever," is not sufficient faith for healing. It must be a specific faith, given by God, for the individual case as we pray concerning it. This alone is the prayer of faith. This alone is the faith of God which brings healing as distinguished from our own self-efforts at faith, which brings only disappointment, self deception, and false claims to that which we have not really experienced. We recall an illustration of this truth which some years ago came under our own notice. A number of friends had gathered at the call of one of the group, to pray for a fellow friend who was lying at the point of death in a distant mission field. As we prayed with increasing earnestness there came into our hearts a marked, conscious spirit of assurance and confidence that our prayer had been heard and answered. One month after came the tidings by letter that although the family of the sick man had gathered at his bedside several times, to see him die, yet a short time after the day on which we had received the assurance from God of his recovery he had been suddenly restored to health and was then about his usual duties. Not long after we were called to the room of a young friend whose eyes were also turned toward the foreign field, but who was being hindered by ill-ness. We prayed, again and again for him. At last, after an hour of supplication on his behalf, we arose from our knees without a shadow of assurance concerning his recovery. We could get no liberty save in resting in submission to God's will, whatever that might be. In one week the young man had gone home to be with the Lord. We had all faith in God's ability to heal tile last named friend as well as the first. But we had no assurance of faith from God that He would do so. The lesson seemed clear In one case it was God's will to heal; in the other it was not.

The supreme truth therefore which must be writ large over this whole question of healing is – *the Sovereignty of God.* If, when we come to Him in prayer for healing, it be His will to heal, He will give us the assurance of the same and enable us to offer the prayer of faith, which faith, being given by Himself, is at once the promise and pledge of answer. But if it is not His will to so heal, then, as in all prayer, it is simply ours to suffer patiently whatever He permits to come, and to miss none of its blessing through failure of submission.

A word as to the anointing with oil mentioned in this same passage in James. The oil is plainly the symbol of the Holy Spirit, as the sole agent in healing. The formal anointing of the sick honors God in acknowledging Him as the healer as well as creator of the body. Doubtless it pleases Him to have His children, when so led, give this testimony to Him, in sickness. On the other hand the many cases in which He heals without this rite show that anointing is but the shadow of which the Holy Spirit is the substance. And just as God baptizes with the Holy Spirit, without the water baptism with which He usually associates it in the Word, so does He heal myriads without the anointing here named. We are evidently to use it when the Holy Spirit leads us to it. We are plainly not to be in bondage to it as having any efficacy in itself apart from the Holy Spirit it typifies. The same interpretation of (be Spirit, rather than the letter of this passage, would lead us to believe that where, for any reason, the elders of the church were not available, the calling of godly friends who knew the Lord in prayer, would satisfy all needful conditions as to the persons who were engaged in this fellowship of prayer for the sick.

* * * *

Does God USE means in healing?

There are two classes of believers who are in error here: —

Those who look to God and rule out means.
Those who look to means and rule out God.

Let us consider them in their order: –

1. Those who look to God and ignore means.

Two principles may be laid down here concerning healing: –

First, there are three forms of healing: –

The Supernatural. – This explains itself. It is that form of healing in which God Himself, without the use of means, and by the direct touch of His own omnipotence, heals the body.

The Natural. – Where health returns through rest, sleep, nourishing food, change of scene, and a ceasing from the violation of those natural laws by the transgression of which health has been lost, and through the observance of which it again returns.

The Remedial. – Where remedies and mean, either medical or surgical, are concerned in the restoration to health

Second, all healing is divine healing; God alone heals. No physician will claim that medicines or remedies heal. They furnish a means upon which the healing life force within lays hold and uses in the process of healing, but they them-selves do not heal. And back of all such life is the God of life, who alone heals, for only He who is the creator of life can restore and renew it when impaired. Thus, whether healing is supernatural,

natural, or remedial, it is God who is back of it all, and working through it all. Therefore if God is thus back of, and makes use of, all these forms of healing it is for God alone and not us to decide which form He shall use. It is not for me, the patient, but for God, the physician, to decide whether means shall be used or not. Wherefore no Christian man dare say "I will not use means," lest he may be thereby saying, "I will not obey God." To look to God only and refuse all means, is to confine God to the supernatural and rule Him out of the natural. But God will not have it so. For what we call the natural, is simply God working through the natural. And for us to condemn the natural and insist upon the supernatural in the answers to our prayers for the body is simply to dictate to God that He shall act in one way and not in another. The natural is God's ordinary way of working, the supernatural His extraordinary way of working. If it is wholly a matter for God as to whether He will heal, it must be wholly for God to choose how He will heal. It is not for us to choose what we shall do, but to do what God shall choose.

What then shall we do here? Simply this. Suppose God gives us, in prayer, assurance of His will to heal. Then let us wait upon Him in prayer and communion until He shows us by His Spirit what He would have us to do. Then "Whatsoever He saith unto you, do it." If He leads us to trust Him for supernatural deliverance without the intervention of men, or means, let us so do. If He guides us to some human instrument or means let us receive it as from Him and trust Him in the natural as well as the supernatural. It is for God to choose. It is for us to trust and obey. And in it all if our expectation is from Him we shall never be disappointed.

2. Those who look to means only and ignore God.

Why is this a mistake? And why should we go to God in prayer concerning sickness?

I. *Because of Obedience.* – "Is any among you afflicted? let him pray. Is any among you cheerful? (R. V.) let him sing psalms. Is any sick among you? let him," etc. Just as the cheerful were to sing praises, so the sick and afflicted were to pray. "The body is for the Lord, and the Lord for the body." Therefore it honors God and pleases Him for us to bring to Him in prayer everything which concerns that body. It is a simple step of obedience to the Word of God: A simple conformity to the command of God that "in all things with prayer and supplication, we should make known our requests unto Cod."

II. *Because of Teaching.* – The body is the temple of the Holy Ghost, the dwelling place of God, and should be regarded and used as such. Yet how many believers fail to so treat it. We are daily transgressing the laws which are created for its good. We live to eat, instead of eating to live; we over-work and under-rest; we chafe and fret; we abuse in numberless ways the wonderful temple in which God dwells. "For this cause, says Paul, speaking of like transgressions, "many are weak and sickly among you." (I Cor. ii : 30.) Much of our sickness is due to abuse of our bodies in various ways; is the natural result of violation of its laws. God would teach us His own lessons concerning these things, and have us walk in physical as well as spiritual obedience and holiness.

Then, too, there are lessons of submission, of purification, and of patience to be learned in this selfsame school. It is for this reason that He calls us to come to Him in prayer, in sickness, that we may see and learn and obey these lessons and "perfect our holiness in the fear of the Lord," both in the body and in the Spirit.

III. Because of Healing. – The man who looks to means only, and ignores God in sickness, may, by neglect of prayer, be losing one of the greatest blessings of his life. To miss prayer may be to miss a miracle of healing. For it may be God's will to heal by supernatural touch, instead of means. This, as we have seen, is for God to decide. And we can only learn His will, and know His omnipotent power in healing, as we come to Him in prayer. The church of God is losing much here. Because of the erroneous teaching concerning divine healing, she has swung to the other extreme and is practically and daily denying the power of God to heal at all in these latter days. But God is the same mighty God as of old. The days of miracles are not any more past than the days of His omnipotent power are past.

It is surely a symptom of waning faith that so many of God's own children should scout the bare thought of God healing by supernatural power in these days. Yet such mighty deeds at His hands are as much needed to-day as they ever were, both to strengthen the faith of His children, and, as a sign, to attest His omnipotent power to an unbelieving world. If God's children always came to Him in prayer concerning sickness there would be many more cases of marvelous healing to the glory of His name than the church now sees. Granted that the man who trusts God only, and rules out all means is in error. Yet the Christian who trusts means only and rules out God is just as much in error. If the first man confines God to the supernatural, the second limits Him to the natural. He insists that God work through second causes only. He comes to see only the means and is blind to the God back of the means. To neglect God's teaching concerning divine healing, because men's teaching is marred by error, may be to miss untold blessing from our lives, and to fall into a trap which has been set for us by no less an adversary than the enemy of our souls himself.

VIII. PRAYER AND COMMUNION

Through Communion the Spirit of God anoints us with the life of God.

With that point is knit up closely our description of communion, and that is the daily looking unto Jesus for the continuous inflow of His Divine life.

Life comes through looking. Have you ever noticed the beautiful connection between the story of the Israelites in the wilderness, bitten with serpents, and looking for life to that serpent, and John 3:14, 15, in which our Lord comments upon the same? As we read the story of the dying Israelites, we are told that they were bidden to look unto the serpent, and they would receive life, and that as they looked the life came. Now, the Holy Ghost, in speaking of regeneration, takes up this illustration, and goes on to say that "as Moses lifted up the serpent in the wilderness even so must the Son of Man be lifted up, that whosoever" – you would think from the illustration that what would follow would be "that whosoever looketh unto Him" – because that is the picture of the wilderness illustration. But instead of that the Divine writer by a quick turn of the metaphor says "that whosoever believeth in Him should receive eternal life." What is the suggestion, what is the thought here? That believing in Jesus in simply looking unto Jesus for life. And the simplest thought concerning faith, and the most beautiful description of it for your mind and mine, is simply that thought of the Israelite expectantly looking unto the serpent for life. That is what faith is. Faith is not a thing. Faith is not an emotion. Faith is an attitude, a posture. Faith is looking unto Jesus for life.

Now, as by the act of faith we receive life; by the daily, continuous attitude of faith by which we mean communion, we constantly receive the inflowing life of the Lord Jesus Christ.

Just as at the moment we expectantly look unto Jesus Christ in faith, we receive life, so all through our life we are to continue looking to Jesus Christ in the place of communion for the continuous anointing with the life of God. "Except a man drink My blood, he has no life." And what was His blood? "The blood is the life." And Jesus meant that just as a man was refreshed and life came unto him day by day by constant drinking, so a man in his spiritual walk must be constantly drinking of the life of Jesus Christ, in the secret place of prayer, of communion.

This simple thought of looking unto Jesus it the core thought of communion with our Lord. As men who are spiritually dead in ourselves, that is, in our old nature, and who are dependent on the life of Jesus Christ down-flowing from heaven, we are to be looking unto our living Jesus in these moments of communion in the solitude of our own closet, and keep drinking His life, as a man drinks water to refresh his soul.

Here is a man who has an endorser upon his note. The man who has given the note fails, and becomes bankrupt. His creditors begin to threaten him. One day there comes to him the rich man who has endorsed his note and says: "Now, don't trouble; don't be concerned; just look to me to pay that note when it matures. You have no funds; you have no resources; you are helpless. All I ask is that you keep looking unto me" Henceforth that man is simply looking to his endorser, and when the note comes due, with nothing to meet it, and himself utterly helpless, it is paid. This is a picture of our need of communion. In ourselves we are spiritual bankrupts. While we receive the life of God at conversion, yet in ourselves we are utterly dependent upon Jesus Christ moment by moment for the anointing of His life, and as we look to Him in the place of communion, His life does somehow flow into us. We, as God's children, will acknowledge that of all the things of which we are conscious after the hour of prayer, and in the hour of prayer, the consciousness of the presence of God's Spirit in our hearts is the most real and blessed. In prayer, as nowhere else, do we realize His presence, and out from the place of prayer, anointed and refreshed by His presence, we come forth feeling that the life of the Lord has really touched our souls.

This, then, is the blessedness of communion – that in communion we really, as Christ says drink His spiritual life. You may say it is mystical. True, all life is mystical, nor can we understand it. But you know it is a fact; you know that your own soul is quickened and refreshed by communion, and Christ interprets that quickening when He says that it is His life, the life of His Spirit, that thus touches and refreshes us.

* * * *

Through Communion the Spirit of God reveals

TO US THE MIND OF GOD.

In Rev. 1: 10, we read: "I was in the Spirit on the Lord's Day, and I heard a voice." Why did John hear the voice? Because he was in the Spirit. Because John was in the place of communion, the place of waiting upon God, and because being in the Spirit, anointed with the Spirit, the Spirit of God who takes of the thing of God and reveals them unto us, could show them unto John. It is in the place of prayer and the place of communion that the Spirit of God is able to show us the things of God. "I was in the Spirit," and – "I heard a voice." Do we not often lack the knowledge of God's will? And is it not because we do not put ourselves into that atmosphere in which the Spirit of God alone can reveal Himself; because our spiritual ears are not attuned by communion to hear the voice by which the Spirit of God would speak to us? Do we not miss much of the revelation of God's will because we are not in the place above all other places where God reveals that will – the place of prayer, the place of communion? We cannot hear the voice because we do not shut ourselves apart in the only place where we can hear it.

On the shores of Lake Huron, one day, last summer, a little group of us were standing on the dock awaiting the arrival of the steamer. All about us was a babel of voices. Presently the young clerk said: "Come into the fish house." (It was a fishing village, and there was a little warehouse where they packed their fish.) We went in with him, and he shut the door, and said: "Listen!" As we stood there we could plainly hear the sound of the approaching boat – the peculiar intermittent beating of the paddles of a side-wheel steamer. Then we walked out of the door to the wharf where the people were talking, and again the sound of the approaching steamer vanished. Again with a friend we went into the room, and again we heard it clearly and plainly. We were in the place of stillness. There were no voices about to distract, or disturb, or break the silence, and there we could distinctly hear the approaching steamer. We went out and sat down upon the wharf, and in few minutes the smoke from her funnels arose above the island. "What a lesson!" we thought. When we get alone in the chamber of communion with God, we can hear the voice of God; God can reveal His mind to us as nowhere else. But we miss that mind, and we miss that guidance, and we fail to hear that voice, because in the hubbub and distraction of life we are in surroundings where the Spirit, who speaks with a still, small voice, cannot make known to us His will. Who of us is not familiar with this fact of the out- flashing of truth upon the mind in or after prayer? Is there a man who has ever prayed for guidance and has not been conscious that this guidance came in or after prayer? Something would flash upon us, some word of God, some incident in our life that would suddenly open to us the guidance we wanted, and say to us: "This is the path; walk ye in it." And when we came to find out where that guidance came, it was in prayer, or after prayer. It is in communion that God flashes upon us the light of His own will, the revelation of His own mind.

We remember meeting a friend, after his return from South Africa, where he had been visiting one known the world over for his close walk with his Lord. "What is the secret of his great power?" His reply was: "Communion. He seems always to be in communion with God." He said: "I will illustrate: When I went to see him, a minister from this country handed me a New Testament, saying: 'Will you ask Mr. – to write a sentiment in that Testament for me?' After I had been there a few days I stated the request of the ministerial brother. Mr. – took the New Testament and said: 'Well, I must go aside awhile.' He walked over into the corner of the room and sat down in an alcove, waiting on the Lord. Then I saw him write, and when he came back to me, the verse on the flyleaf of the Testament was: 'The Son can do nothing of Himself, but what He seeth the Father do.' I took that book home, and by the grace of God that minister's life was well nigh transformed from that simple verse – 'The Son can do nothing of Himself.' "

"Ah, we thought, there is the secret. We would have taken the book and written down the first sentence which came into our mind, but this man who knows the Lord, as few men do, and knows the mind of the Lord as revealed in communion and prayer, went apart to get that mind. Then when he wrote the sentence it was the Lord's sentence, and went home to the heart and the life of the man who received it. God help us to wait in communion to get the mind of God, that the words we give to men may be the words of God, and give birth to the blessed life of God in them.

* * * *

Through Communion the Spirit of God TRANSFORMS US INTO THE IMAGE OE GOD.

Notice the reference in 2 Cor. 3:18. Opposite that verse in our Bible are these words: "God's photograph gallery." You who know something of photography, know there are three things needful in it. First, there is the object which is to be photographed. Second, there is a sensitive plate that must look toward that object and receive the impression of it. Third, there is the sunshine which transfers the object to the sensitive plate. As we read that verse one day we thought: "Surely it is God's photograph gallery." Listen to it: "But we all with open face" – there is the sensitive plate turned toward the Lord. We all with open face "beholding as in a glass the glory of the Lord" There is the object to be photographed: – "He hath foreordained us to be conformed into the image of His Son." Listen again: "We all with open face beholding as in a glass the glory of the Lord, are changed" —there is the process – "from glory to glory." In what way? "Even as by the Spirit of the Lord." There like the sunshine is the marvelous power that transfers the image to you and to me. Transformed through beholding; transformed through "looking unto Jesus." What a wonderful thought it is! And it is in this place of communion, as we look unto Him, that this transformation takes place.

You have heard the story of the sea and the cloud. The sea looked up into the heavens and saw the beauty of the great white summer clouds, and longed to become a cloud. So it struggled, and strove, and tossed itself into the air, and dashed itself against the rocks, but all to no purpose. And then the sun looked down upon the sea, and said: "Be quiet; be still; and just look unto me. And then the tossing sea grew quiet, and ceased its strivings, and lay there with open face beholding the glory of the sun. And as it did so, the sun steadily, moment by moment, drew, and changed, and transformed the sea, until bye and bye, in the heavens was another cloud in all its beauty. What the sea could not do with all its striving, the sun did, simply through the sea's looking unto it. And so too we struggle and strive, and work to become like Jesus, but somehow – we do not know how; we do not understand any more than we understand how that beautiful picture is transferred from the landscape to the plate – as we look unto Jesus in the place of prayer; as we look unto Him in the place of communion; as our souls cease their strivings and their vain struggles to make the old flesh life like Him – which can never be, – and just look, helplessly, to Him, somehow we are changed into the image of the Lord Jesus Christ. As we look unto Jesus we come to look like Jesus. Those who wait upon Him shine with His glory. When Moses came out of the mountain, his face was shining with the glory of God. Why? Because he had gazed into the face of God for forty days. And when he came down, he stood a transfigured man before the people, with the image of God in his face, so that he had to cover it, for they could not bear looking upon it. How beautiful then is it that as we took unto Jesus, we are transformed into the image of Jesus. That even down here in the dark night of faith, somehow or other, we grow like Him. The moment a man perfectly sees Jesus, that moment a man is going to be perfectly like Jesus. "When He shall appear, we shall be like Him, for we shall see Him as He is" – "we shall be like Him, for we shall see Him." Through the imperfect glass of faith, the likeness is imperfect. With the perfect face-to-face vision, the image shall be perfect. Here the picture is being taken in a cloudy day, "through a glass darkly." It takes long time-exposures, and the work seems to be slow. Then it will be an instantaneous flash, and "we shall be like Him." In an instant, "in a moment, in the twinkling of an eye" – the Lord, the glory, the likeness! Thanks be unto God. We are waiting for that glad moment. The instant we see Jesus Christ face to face, that instant we will be changed into the glory of Jesus Christ. And just so far as we see Him now in communion, so far are we made like Him, even down here.

* * * *

Through Communion the Spirit of God fits us for the service of God.

Do we say communion is passive? Do we say a busy man has no time to spend in communion? You may live along the line of a great railroad for many years and yet notice that it does not make any difference how the freight yards are congested with traffic, or how occupied the train men are with their various duties, those great freight and passenger engines are never too busy to stop for coal and water. And why? Because fuel and water mean power. So the man who says he is too busy to spend time in communion with God simply says he is too busy to have power with God. And as that whole great railroad system would be tied up with helpless, "dead" locomotives, as the railroad men call them, if they did not stop long enough to get power, even so a great deal of our Christian work is tied up with helpless, lifeless Christians, because they do not stop long enough to get the power of God.

We are told of Gabriel, that when he came to Zacharias, he said: "I am Gabriel, which stand in the presence of God, and I am sent" Do we say that it is a passive life to wait before God in communion? It is those that wait before Him who are sent by Him. No man is fitted to look into the face of men in service until he has looked into the face of God in communion. And we are told (Rev. 8:2), that to the seven angels that stood before God the trumpets were given. "Passive business," we say, just standing there before God, these seven angels looking into His face!" But it was to these that the execution of His will was committed. Oh, when we remember that looking unto Him in communion, as we have seen, reveals His mind, impresses His image, fills with His life, and gives His power, then, who is so fitted to go forth and fake the messages of God and do the service of God as the man who is transformed into the image of God, filled with the life of God, and knows the will of God? That is why communion fits us for the service of God.

When David Brainerd had spent eight days in the heart of the forest praying to God to pour out His life upon the benighted savages, among whom he was laboring, he came forth to speak the Word of God. He did not know the language and had therefore to speak through an interpreter. To his distress he found that this interpreter was intoxicated. And yet through that drunken interpreter the power of God was so poured out through His anointed servant, that scores of those savages came to Jesus Christ under the power of his ministry. Ah! If we would be used to touch men with the power of God, we must be much in the place of communion with God. And by His grace as we go forth into the world, shall we not live the higher Life in the best sense of the word, and the Spirit of God will surely fill us with the life of God; reveal to us the will of God; transform us into the image of God; and send us forth with the power of God.

Made in the USA
Middletown, DE
22 September 2020